THE SMELL OF REEVES AND MORTIMER

THE
SMELL
OF
REEVES
AND
MORTIMER

Vic Reeves & Bob Mortimer

Dedicated to
Alice May Moir

and

with unqualified gratitude to
John Birkin and Charlie Higson

FANTAIL BOOKS
Published by the Penguin Group
Penguin Books Ltd, 27 Wrights Lane, London W8 5TZ, England
Penguin Books USA Inc., 375 Hudson Street, New York, New York 10014, USA
Penguin Books Australia Ltd, Ringwood, Victoria, Australia
Penguin Books Canada Ltd, 10 Alcorn Avenue, Toronto, Ontario,Canada M4V 3B2
Penguin Books (NZ) Ltd, 182–190 Wairau Road, Auckland 10, New Zealand

Penguin Books Ltd, Registered Offices: Harmondsworth, Middlesex, England

First published 1993
1 3 5 7 9 10 8 6 4 2

Set in 12/16pt Linotype Frutiger by Goodfellow & Egan Ltd, Cambridge
Made and printed in Great Britain by William Clowes Limited, Beccles and London

Reeves and Mortimer was first transmitted on BBC 2
on 21 September 1993

The video of the series is distributed by BBC Enterprises and
is available from all good stockists

SHOW

OPENING TITLES

Yarn *(Over titles, voice-over by Patrick Allen)*

Austria 1930. A young boy is challenged by his mischievous grandfather to attempt to throw a handbell at the local village idiot.

Readily taking up the challenge, the excited youth hurls the bell across the sun-soaked village square with all his might. Onlookers adjust their lederhosen and swiftly drain their elaborate flip-topped bier steins as they follow the flight of the golden bell through the air in terrified anticipation of imminent contact 'twixt a bell and an idiot.

Subsequently ostracized by the local community and exiled to Wales, ladies and gentlemen, please welcome the grandfather and his unruly charge . . . Reeves & Mortimer.

Vic and Bob prance (glide) on to stage from opposite sides and 'pipette' centre stage, shouting the familiar words 'hello and good evening'.

In the background and understandably never picked out by the camera, is a hunchback with a long curved yellow beak wearing a leotard and carrying a placard with the rude word 'bra' on it. He walks slowly across backstage with an understandably bizarre limp.

SONG: 'THE WINDMILLS OF YOUR MIND'

To the music of the original Noel Harrison hit . . . BUT . . . and it's a big one . . . the arrangement must kick off with a big, blustery Hollywood showbiz Jack Parnell big band bonanza. Then say after forty seconds AND ONLY THEN does the music quieten down to the style of original, and even then, as the song matures, entices and disturbs, there is a gradual build of sound until the final deafening crescendo, when kettledrum collides with trombone and the smouldering embers of an oppressed people engulf the stage. The final chorus is, however, so gentle and moving that any normal man or woman must surely shed a single saline tear.

Now the words of the song are illustrated by Vic's drawings, which are displayed on a giant projection screen to the rear of the set. Whilst singing the words, the comedians simply stand by the screen, gazing upon the images.

However, at the beginning of the song and end, the comedians comically dance around the following items:

- *2 × kitchen chairs that the boys climb on and collapse in the Fred Astaire mode*
- *2 × 18" high, 12" wide white pipes that the boys can put a foot in*
- *1 × trampet*
- *A 12" high 10ft wide wall*

Like a shrimp in a suitcase on a window ledge
Like a pair of tartan slippers underneath a hedge
Like a scoutmaster at daybreak putting peanuts
    in his glove
Like a specially formed ice arch for climbing over
    doves
Like a sardine with a hairnet staring at a priest.

Chorus
These things we always find
in the windmills of your mind.

Like a sugar unicycle being ridden by a fork
Like a battenburg owned by Jesus that
    miraculously can talk
Like a lemon pip with sideboards fighting a
    bearded crab
Like Bono in a boob tube on a choir-master's lap
Like an elaborate heating system apparently in
    Kent.

Chorus

These things we always find
in the windmills of your mind.

Like a badger with an afro throwing sparklers at
    the Pope
Like a family of foxes glowering at some soap
Like a lump of Nazi nougat walking down an
    avenue
Like a Tudor vacuum cleaner saying how do you
    do
Like a kestrel having sex above a television set.

Chorus

These things we always find
in the windmills of your mind.

VIC & BOB

*At the end of the song Vic and Bob proceed to
their understandably double-seated desk (see
drawing of desk overleaf for a much deeper
understanding of this double-seated Dougal
bench).*

*Vic and Bob formally introduce themselves to
each other and the audience and then perform
the following jokes.*

VIC   Good evening.

BOB   I was going to say that.

VIC   Well, go on.

SET

1. PLAIN BACKGROUND (WHITE) WITH HUGE R&M IN BLACK ON THE BACK IN BLACK

2. HUGE DORIC COLUMNS ACTING AS TABS .THESE,VIA THE GIFT OF OPTICAL ILLUSION MAKE THE LETTERS LOOK EVEN BIGGER THAN THEY ACTUALLY ARE.

3. THE INNER LINE OF THE UPRIGHT SECTION OF THE 'R' WILL ACT AS A TAB,INVISIBLE FROM THE FRONT AS IS THE INNER LINE OF THE 'M' CENTRE STAGE . NB. CAMERAS SHOOTING FROM SIDE OF STAGE(ie 42S)MEANS THAT THE 'R' SEMI CIRCLE MUST BE ELONGATED TO ACCOMMODATE.

4. SEPERATE AREA FOR BAND SO THEY ARE ONLY SEEN IF REQUIRED

THE DESK IS SITUATE CENTRE REAR OF STAGE USEFULLY ALLOWING THE "R & M" LOGO TO PROVIDE BOTH A DRAMATIC BACKGROUND AND A SENSE OF THE POWER AND THE NIGHT OF THE GREAT ROMAN EMPIRE.(SAMSONITE LUGGAGE)

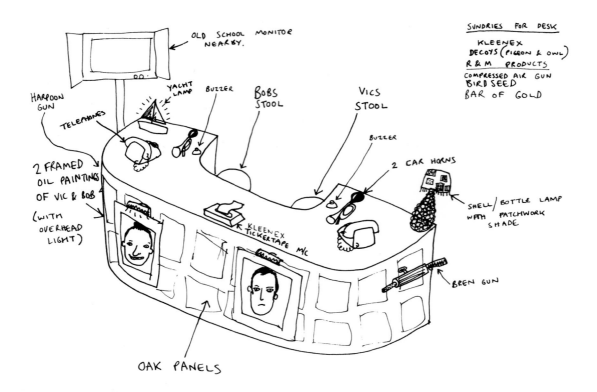

OLD SCHOOL MONITOR NEARBY.

SUNDRIES FOR DESK
KLEENEX
DECOYS (PIGEON & OWL)
R & M PRODUCTS
COMPRESSED AIR GUN
BIRD SEED
BAR OF GOLD

HARPOON GUN

TELEPHONES

YACHT LAMP

BUZZER

BOBS STOOL

VICS STOOL

BUZZER

2 CAR HORNS

2 FRAMED OIL PAINTINGS OF VIC & BOB

(WITH OVERHEAD LIGHT)

SHELL/BOTTLE LAMP WITH PATCHWORK SHADE

KLEENEX
TICKERTAPE M/C

BREN GUN

OAK PANELS

BOB   No point now.

VIC   Try and get your petty complaints in quicker. Look at your script.

BOB   I haven't got one.

VIC   WHAT!

BOB   Well, I got these. (*Holds up shite.*)

VIC   That's not script.

BOB   Only kiddin', I've got script here with only one line on it.

VIC   What is it?

BOB   Good evening. (*Laugh mode.*)

VIC   Can you smell onions?

BOB   No.

VIC   Not even if you're right close up?

VIC   What's that on your face?

BOB   Skin.

VIC   Would you like a bite of my juicy Granny Smith apple?

BOB   Yes . . . (*But, oh, it was simply a partly inflated green balloon.*)

VIC   Have you seen my watch? (*Holding out naked wrist.*)

BOB   You're not wearing one!

VIC   No, I was simply enquiring as to whether you had seen my watch whilst simultaneously displaying to you my wrist.

VIC   Have you seen today's copy of the Express? (*Holds up picture of 125 inter-city express train.*)

VIC   Waiter, there is an animal in my soup!

BOB   No, sir, that is Alan Price who left the Animals in order to follow a solo career and star in films.

Cue heavy drumbeat. Vic and Bob play along on airdrums.

At the end of the last funny joke Vic and Bob are seen alternately and in extreme close-up laughing with wide open mouths and childish enquiring eyes. (This laughter could potentially be pre-recorded to enhance strangeness of this funny visual gag.)

VIC   'Eee we're havin' a laugh, aren't we?

BOB   Yeah.

Repeat the aforementioned funny visual gag.

VIC   Later on we will be meeting . . .

BOB   the Watermark Sisters . . . You can only see them if you hold them up to the light.

VIC   A man who is part banister and he's going to slide down himself.

BOB   And, of course, Uncle Peter.

Enter Uncle Peter. Vic and Bob don't see him.

VIC   You haven't booked Uncle Peter, when did he get out then?

BOB   Well, he's out specially to appear on the show – give us a break.

UNCLE PETER   Donkey, ee aw. Dog, woof bark. Donkey . . .

VIC   What, there's a fight going on? *(Stands.)*

UNCLE PETER   *(pointing over to the right)* Donkey, ee aw.

BOB   Two sailors having a fight where? *(Stands.)*

UNCLE PETER   Over there.

VIC   Oh, this is ridiculous, fighting on the first show. *(Throws down cup and saucer.)*

BOB   Come on, let's sort it out.

Vic and Bob march over to fighting men chanting 'fight, fight'.

FIGHTING MEN

They are aged 58 and 61. They are very thin and white skinned. They are wearing interesting dress (see drawing), and are stood on separate blocks of frozen kitten piddle. (NB The fighting men are not revealed to the audience until Vic and Bob commence their walk over to them.)

VIC   Eh, what's the problem here?

1ST FIGHTER   My good friend the ordinary seaman Mick Box here claims that all apples have pips.

2ND FIGHTER   Whereas my colleague able seaman Lee Kerslake is adamant that no apple is pipped.

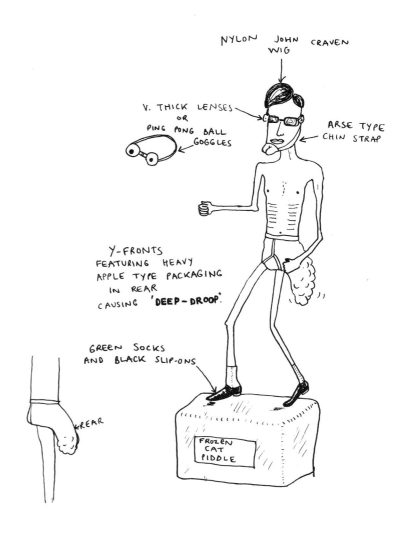

NYLON JOHN CRAVEN WIG

V. THICK LENSES
OR
PING PONG BALL GOGGLES

ARSE TYPE CHIN STRAP

Y-FRONTS FEATURING HEAVY APPLE TYPE PACKAGING IN REAR CAUSING 'DEEP-DROOP'.

GREEN SOCKS AND BLACK SLIP-ONS

REAR

FROZEN CAT PIDDLE

NB *These voices are pre-recorded and not in sync with the actors' mouths.*

Vic and Bob do not know the answer to this. Vic has the bright idea of telephoning Otis Redding for the answer.

OTIS AND MARVIN

Via the gift of satellite link we see Otis (Vic) and Marvin Gaye (Bob) sitting on a dockside wall. They have tiny bodies and legs which are understandably gently kicking in the breeze. Interestingly they have pathetic mithering Northern accents.

VIC   All right, Otis, what are you up to?

OTIS   I'm just sitting here watching the ships coming in . . .

OTIS AND MARVIN   And going out again . . .

OTIS   With my friend Marvin Gaye.

BOB   Otis, can you tell us if apples have pips?

OTIS   Oh Bob, now you're asking a difficult question. You should be asking my friend Gladys Knight. She knows her pips. I do know that celery is quite stringy . . . But I can't help you, I just sit here watching the ships coming in . . .

OTIS AND MARVIN   And going out again . . .

OTIS   Here, I'll ask Marvin if he knows. Marvin, do you know if apples have pips? *(Turns very slowly to Marvin.)*

MARVIN   Well, I've had apples with pips and some without.

OTIS   Well there's your answer, some do. Some don't.

Vic confirms this information with the two fighters whose voices have been pre-recorded. Their lips are clearly out of sync, as are Vic's.

1ST FIGHTER   How can I ever apologize?

2ND FIGHTER   Forgive me also. By way of an apology let me take you to France, where horsemeat is readily available from most butchers.

1ST FIGHTER   Yes and the patisserie are open as late as ten o'clock.

Fighters embrace.

VIC   Sounds great, lads, but don't forget to check out the marvellous street theatre and bars around the Pompidou Centre.

At this point Vic goes into a dream and a dreamy wipe is utilized over the words Pompidou Centre.

CAPED FIGURES

CUT TO   Feet walking along pavement (wearing black Victorian trousers and black shoes with spats). An aston reads 'Paris 1890'.

CUT TO   Rear view of cloaked man with top hat carrying a cane who is opening the door of a French café.

CUT TO   Interior of French café as viewed from the eyes of the caped figure. There are six Frenchmen stood at the bar.

CUT TO   Close-up of caped figure's cane smashing decorative lamp on café table. This shot is repeated a number of times in both slow and fast speed to give the impression of a magnificent and vibrant incident.

CUT TO   The men at the bar all turn at the insistence of the magnificent lamp incident. The bar goes quiet.

CUT TO   Men at bar from caped man's viewpoint. We can see his cane pointing towards the men.

1ST MAN   Huh moi?

Cane shakes to indicate 'not you'.

2ND MAN   Eh moi?

Cane declines him.

3RD MAN   Moi?

Cane waves violently and smashes another lamp – or man with pan on head – then points impatiently and violently towards the men.

All the men say 'Aah' then part to reveal a man behind the bar seen from behind. He is cleaning glasses. This man slowly turns and the camera closes in to reveal that he has a cauliflower for a head.

A flashing aston appears bottom right of screen saying: 'Cauliflower'.

The dream-style wipe is again utilized and we hear Bob pathetically crying 'Help, help'. This 'wakes up' Vic who crosses the stage to find out what is wrong with Bob.

BOB IN MANTRAP

On arrival we see that Bob is trapped in a large mantrap.

Vic asks Bob what's the matter. Bob pathetically explains that his cuff button is hanging off and is about to drop. Vic rushes over to where he sees a child's handy fishing-net. He spots a frantic MAN UNDER THE ICE and gets his permission to take the net and rushes back and holds the net under the button, waiting for it to drop. Vic and Bob wait patiently for a period, exchanging sad, resigned looks with each other and the camera.

At this point Uncle Peter enters. He passes Bob a note. We hear Bob read out the letter (pre-recorded in his mind). It reads: 'Stop fannying

about waiting for that button to drop of Vic's jacket and get on with it . . . Signed Mother.'

BOB   *(still in thought)* Vic's jacket!

On realizing it's Vic's jacket, Bob immediately declares he's not bothered about the button any more. In fact, he hates buttons and starts pulling them off. Vic joins in the fun declaring that he has no time for sleeves and starts ripping the sleeves off. They have a good time ripping them to shreds ending with Vic pouring beetroot, blackcurrant, blood, sweat, coolant, etc., on the jacket. While Vic is stamping on the jacket he notices the name tab on it and understandably chases Bob off stage in a foul temper.

Uncle Peter is left alone on stage. He picks up a Victorian wash jug and looks inside it.

CUT TO   Pre-recording of Uncle Peter looking into jug viewed from inside the jug. He utters the hilarious word 'ooouurrgha'.

UNCLE PETER'S BAND

CUT TO   Uncle Peter playing a child's-size drum-kit, accompanied by Vic and Bob in padded leotards, silver foil peaked caps and ping-pong eyes. Vic has a guitar, Bob has maracas. They sing 'Doo pe dopy da'. They are in front of a cloth backdrop saying: 'The Uncle Peter Band'.

On Uncle Peter's drum kit is written 'Uncle Peter'.

The band sing the following song:

UNCLE PETER   I want to go into neutral, but I'm not in me car.

VIC   Well, bring the car in here,

BOB   And shift it out of gear.

VIC & BOB   Yes, Peter, yes, that is what we'll do.

At the end of the song Peter lets out a haunting

wail and raises his hands to confirm that he has lost his gloves.

CUT TO   Peter's face retracting from the jug. He slowly walks off stage.

FOOD AND DRINK

Cue title animation announcing the arrival of Food and Drink. *This title features a turtle with a human hand pulling the cork out of a bottle of champagne (champers!). The cork flies out knocking a vicar off his ladder and into a Lancashire hot-pot being stirred by a giraffe with a human hand and arm.*

The titles read:

FOOD AND DRINK
introduced by Chris Kelly

The set resembles the real Food and Drink *set. The only prop is a secondary school dining table with tubular steel legs and a wood veneer top. On this table is an 18 inch high Minnie Mouse soft toy surrounded by four battery operated and distressed human hands.*

Chris Kelly (see drawing) is wearing a box of PG Tips and half an Edam Gaffer taped on to his head. His face is obscured by a slice of white Mother's Pride with eye and mouth holes in it secured to the face by Sellotape.

He is wearing a casual shirt, tie and jacket. He is crawling on the floor. As he crawls forward his special telescopic trousers stretch, very nearly giving the impression that his legs are 12 foot long.

When his legs are fully extended Chris (previously seen from the side) turns his head to camera:

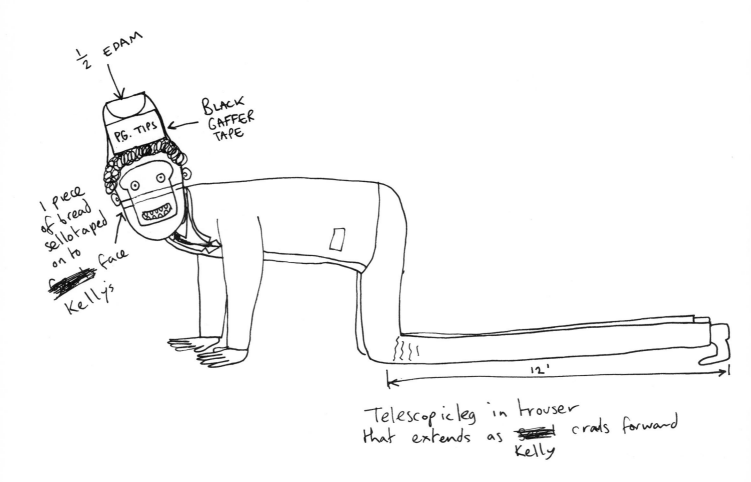

CHRIS   Hello, welcome to *Food and Drink*. This week Jilly and Oz will be sampling some new lightweight pastries. Michael will be cooking some new meat but first here's Derek and Chester with their pick of this week's new booze . . . Derek . . .

CUT TO   Derek and Chester (Vic and Bob) are stood behind a round wooden-legged and red Formica-topped table. On the table are three battery-operated human hands and six anonymous unlabelled bottles of booze.

Bob and Vic are wearing cream and brown checked suits and trilbys.

DEREK   Good evening. Booze first. New booze is this pint of booze here. Chester *(tastes beer)*. Let's have a look at the colour of it *(pours some on table)* . . . Nice brown booze.

CHESTER   What would you drink that booze with?

DEREK   Peanuts, Chester . . . Let's have a look at the colour of the peanuts *(pours peanuts on table)* . . . Nice brown nuts.

CHESTER   Thank you, Derek. Now I've got this new booze *(tastes it)* . . .

DEREK   What is it, Chester?

CHESTER   Plonk . . . Let's have a look at the colour of it *(pours some on table)* . . . Nice piss-coloured plonk.

DEREK   What would you have with that, Chester?

CHESTER   Some of that brown booze, Derek.

At this stage Mike Watton appears with his baby.

MIKE   Have you got any booze for t'baby?

DEREK & CHESTER   You can't give a baby booze.

MIKE   You tight-arsed little monkeys. I'll get me own bloody booze then. *(Mike and baby leave.)*

DEREK   And now here's Jilly and Oz who are trying some of the new season's gases . . .

CUT TO   Jilly and Oz are behind a table. Jilly is much taller than Oz who is only visible from about nipple height upwards. On the table is a can of Ronson lighter fuel, a mound that has been extracted from a marsh and a free-standing gas cooker ring with bunsen burner pipe attached.

JILLY   Thank you, Derek. Yes, the first gas we tried was lighter fuel. *(Jilly takes a deep sniff from the butane can.)*

JILLY   *(breathlessly and searching for her words)*   Mmmmmnnn . . . something for everyone there . . . apples rotting in an old school desk, a dartboard on fire near a toothpick farm, a newt on holiday in Tangier . . . what did you think, Oz?

OZ   I love you.

JILLY   Next we tried marsh gas.

Jilly punctures the marsh mound and we hear gas escaping as the mound deflates . . . Jilly bends down to draw fully from the gas.

JILLY   Mmmnnn . . . meeeeoooow, Oz, that's clouds and poodles' balls, the very lightest of hair that drops from a pensioner following a curly perm, little rabbits throwing cotton wool at a mohair jumper . . . what did you think, Oz?

Jilly looks at Oz and cannot believe her eyes when she sees that he has turned into an owl (a real stuffed one that says 'hoot hoot').

She rubs her eyes as people do when they cannot believe what they are seeing. This does the trick and we see Oz back to normal.

OZ   I love you.

HALLLOOOOOOOO

LIGHT CRUSTS

1. BLONDE
2. LIGHT FLIMSY DRESS
3. FLORAL GARLAND
4. ENGLISH

JILLY

BROWN 'PURVIS'

LADIES MAKE-UP

DENTAL LIP STRETCHER

SELLOTAPE TO PULL EYES WIDE OPEN
OR
ELASTICATED EYE GOGGLES

OZ

JILLY Finally we tried gas mark six. *(Jilly turns on the gas ring and draws deeply from the gas pipe.)*

Ohhhhh . . . a mini moke coming out of your tap driven by a chub lock towing a cowboy boot to the nearest garage, oh . . . oh . . . oh . . . Ozzie.

Again she looks at Ozzie, but finds him to be an owl. She rubs her eyes.

CUT TO   Derek and Chester who suffer from jaw drop and eye bugout as they stare at the bottles of booze in their hands (as if to say 'Wow, deputy, this really is some hot hooch. Boy oh boy oh boy').

CUT TO   Jilly just finishing rubbing her eyes. She now sees Oz as an owl with a machine gun. On seeing this, she collapses backwards on to the floor.

CUT TO   Oz as normal, looking at the floor behind the table.

OZ   I love you.

CUT TO   Chris Kelly. He is still on all fours. We see him side on, facing a two-bar electric fire (the fact that it is a fire is not revealed in this shot). Chris turns to camera and it is revealed that he was facing a fire and that the slice of bread on his face is now toasted. His hair is singed and the PG Tips box is lightly smoking. The Edam is beginning to melt.

CHRIS   And now here's Pete Townsend.

CUT TO   Pete Townsend lookalike (during his white boiler suit and DM boot period). He performs his legendary combination arm windmill guitar stroke and scissor leap.

CUT TO   Chris Kelly, now with a delicious slice of cheese on toast in his hand and just the PG Tips remaining on his head.

CHRIS   Pete Townsend *(takes bite of cheese on*

toast) . . . and thank you to Jean Miller from the coast for this novel way of preparing cheese on toast . . . Next Michael with his new meat and in the meantime I'm going to make a nice pot of tea . . .

Pull back to reveal large aluminium pan on a gas hob on the floor next to Chris. It is full of boiling water. Chris puts his head inside the pan.

CUT TO   Michael, who is wearing a white open-necked shirt and a blue apron with white chalkstripes. His sleeves are rolled up. There is a bit of blood on him. He is stood behind a warped butcher's block. On the table are four stainless steel kidney-shaped dishes with meat in them. Each piece of meat has its own individual price flag (with metal pin) secured on it.

MICHAEL   Thanks, Chris . . . Now I've delved deep within the carcass to get these four new meats for you . . . Now *(holding the flag pin of the first new meat)* . . . For example, this one here I found just under the little horn on the giraffe's head. *(Michael then eats the new meat sample and having nowhere to put the flag pin casually sticks it into his forearm.)*

MICHAEL   Mmmm, that's very sweet. Now this one, would you believe, is the retina from the eye of an elephant seal . . . now that's literally all you need . . . just throw the rest of the smelly thing away . . . it's a big old animal . . . about three or four ton, so you might have to hire a skip from your local council.

He then tastes the retina from the end of the flag stick . . .

Mmnnnn, not bad. You'd need about fifty or sixty of these if you were having it as a fun starter, so best perhaps alert the council dump.

Sticks flag stick casually into arm.

But the tenderest new cut is undoubtedly . . .

The right hands from the trainers of the Didsbury Police Dog Display Team.

Camera pulls back to reveal a queue of dog trainers wearing blue V-neck pullovers, shirts and ties, and police hats. They have had their teeth whitened and are smiling to camera whilst offering their right hands up to Michael to be severed.

The officer at the front of the queue is actually having his hand sawn off by Michael whilst having a pleasant conversation with him.

During the above the camera slowly pulls away and we hear jaunty 1950s music.

Chris Kelly intermittently rears up right in front of camera. His head is red, scalded and blistered (steaming).

During the last 15 seconds the following titles are run:

WRITTEN BY
Rambo

SOUND BY
Van Damm
Dolp Lungman

CAMERAS
Mrs Plum
Foghorn Leghorn
Old King Cole
Old Man River
Old Kent Road

PRODUCED BY
I Can't Believe it's Butter
A Skeleton
Daddy Cool

FILMED LIVE AT
King Cobra's Energy Bar

REEVES AND MORTIMER PRODUCTS

VIC   Right, ladies and gentlemen, I'm sure that you like us worry terribly about home security.

BOB   We do, Vic, and it's harrowing that there are no burglar proof burglar alarms on the market.

VIC   Yes, Bob, but even if there were would you be safe with people like Raffles, Billy the Cat, Dracula and erm . . . Climie Fisher about?

BOB   Oh no, not at all . . . Mind you, Vic, internal bars on windows are effective.

VIC   Ah yes, but they're not attractive, are they?

BOB   No . . . So what's the answer?

At this point Peter walks on pushing the Reeves and Mortimer product display board. On the facing page of the board is a drawing of Licky Kicky the security dog (see drawing).

VIC   Have a look at this, Bob *(indicating Licky Kicky)*. What do you make of that?

BOB   Well, it's a lovely cuddly puppy, Vic, but it wouldn't make me feel secure.

VIC   Correct, Bob. On the face of it it is a gorgeous little doggy woggy and he would doubtless wag his tail and lick your face on your return from a hard day's graft at the cream horn factory.

BOB   I love those cream horns.

VIC   I know, I could just do with one now.

BOB   *(pretending to eat a cream horn)* Mmm . . . gorgeous. Oh, the end's snapped off.

VIC   Oh, stop it . . . we'll drive ourselves mad.

VIC   Anyway, Bob, as you know appearances can be deceptive . . . for this cute doggy is . . . none other than Licky Kicky the robotic security dog . . . He may look cute but I tell you he's a

brute . . . Yes, inserted into Licky's hindquarters are 40 tonnes of sharpened, hardened steel . . . simply pull Licky's tail thus and his hind leg swings out in a scything 40 foot arc killing indiscrimately within an 80 foot radius.

BOB So you simply move the tail to kick and you're safe as houses?

VIC Yep.

Flashing aston appears briefly declaring 'Licky Kicky security system £10.99'.

BOB What if you're not there, say you're at work or on holiday?

Vic realizes his horrible error and is shocked and shamefaced. Bob is embarrassed as he has let the cat out of the bag.

BOB Also from our animal K-wackers Range, (*turning page with his now bleeding right hand*) Quack Quack the Home Brew Duck.

VIC Yes, delicious home-brewed lager in just seven seconds.

BOB That's right. Quacky simply combs ordinary tap water with his 'Alco-comb' and in just seven seconds you're ready to present your guests with refreshing lager.

VIC How does the 'Alco-comb' work, Bob?

BOB I don't know but it does, yes.

VIC & BOB Quack Quack, he's a home brew duck (*sung like a jingle*).

NB *Over this jingle a flashing aston is displayed on screen declaring: 'Quack quack + Alco-comb £199.99'.*

SLADE IN RESIDENCE

Animated titles and music

Interior of Birmingham council house. You know the sort of thing:

- *Brown draylon three-piece suite.*
- *Copper canopy over stone-clad gas fireplace with coal-effect feature.*
- *Copper bedpans and horse brasses and pipes on wall.*
- *MFI shelving units containing porcelain horse and cart, model Cadillac, various common vases, carriage clock, family of pierrot dolls, etc, etc.*
- *Blue and cream swirly nylon carpet.*
- *Orange wool fireside rug.*
- *Nice copper bin with black ship on it.*
- *Orange curtain with things on it and nets over the window.*
- *Dull brown flowery wallpaper.*
- *On the wall a picture of a weeping cretin, a Spitfire plane emerging from cloud cover, and a black sea of oil paint with one yellow and two orange blobs on it representing harbour lights.*
- *A bush teak-veneered TV on legs.*
Etc. etc. etc. etc. etc.

Noddy, Don and Jimmy are sat at the dining table. Noddy has his head tilted to one side. Jimmy and Don are staring at his head. In the manner that one might stare at a 'spot the difference' competition, i.e. quizzically.

JIM   Italy.

NODDY   No.

DON   Germany.

NODDY   No, wrong, Don.

JIM   Africa.

NODDY   Getting warmer.

DON   I've got it . . . Africa.

NODDY   He's just said that.

DON   He did not.

JIM   I did . . . Have another go.

DON   Is it abroad?

NODDY   Don, all countries are abroad these days.

DON   No, they're not . . . Greece isn't abroad.

JIM   He's got a point, Nod.

NODDY   Oh all right. But it's not Greece anyway . . . Come on, you're not trying.

DAVE   *(appears from kitchen with some cutlery with which to set the table for dinner)* Come on, you lot, out of the way, you're always getting under my feet. I want to set the table.

JIM   Oh, Dave, we were playing Guess the Country with Nod.

DAVE   Well, I can't wait around. Come on, Noddy, give them the answer.

NODDY   *(turns to camera. His left sideburn has been teased into the shape of India. Next to the sideburn Nod is holding a postcard-size clear outline of India)* It's India . . . same as

yesterday . . . I get the comfy chair for *Countdown* and exclusive use of the potty . . . and the spoon . . . till *Eastenders*.

JIM & DON   Ohhh.

DAVE   Hold on, who put this glass of Tizer on my nice clean surface?

DON, NODDY & JIM   Don't look at me . . . Not me. *(Etc.)*

DAVE   Right now, one of you did it and you're not getting any dinner till one of you owns up.

They all look sheepish and innocent.

DAVE   Right, that's it, let's smell your breath. *(Smells Don.)* Um Bongo, two white mice, a flying saucer, an ice pop, and a 5lb Cheddar . . . It's not you. *(Smells Jim.)*

DON   I'm clear. I bet it's him . . . Yes, he probably did it on purpose.

JIM   Shut it, Don, or I'll give it to you.

DAVE   Yeah, shut it, Don . . . Now give us a good sniffsworth . . . three quarts of Bovril, an oxtail, a tongue, liver and kidney pudding, trotters, a heart and a 5lb Cheddar . . . You're clear . . . Right then, Noddy, that leaves you. Why don't you just admit it now?

NODDY   You can smell my breath, Dave, I've got nothing to hide . . . go on smell it, smell it, take it in.

DAVE   *(smells Noddy)* Two bottles of cider, 10 pints of beer, 5 bottles of cider, 6 pints of beer, 3 peanuts, another bottle of cider, another bottle of cider, 2 peanuts, 7 pints of beer, a 5lb Cheddar and a Polo mint . . . Wait a minute, Nod, you're trying to disguise the smell of something with that Polo mint.

DON   Yeah, it's the oldest trick in the book.

JIM   Yeah, what else would he be trying to hide if it wasn't the smell of Tizer?

DAVE Right, Noddy, no dinner for you till you've got rid of that stain.

NODDY Look, it wasn't me . . . I can't stand the bloody stuff.

DAVE Get cleaning, Noddy, the sooner it's done the sooner you eat.

JIM Yeah, get cleaning . . . bloody India.

DAVE (*to Don and Jimmy*) Right you two, who wants a Cup-A-Soup?

Jim and Don both raise their hands like eager schoolchildren.

DAVE Right, do you want a piece of bread, a biscuit or crisps with it?

Both Jim and Don immediately raise hands and shout 'crisps'. Three seconds later Noddy shouts out 'biscuit'.

DAVE You'll get nothing till my surface is clean and while you're at it take those library books back as well . . . (*Begins to leave.*)

NODDY Make your mind up. I can't clean the surface and take the library books back at the same time . . . (*droning on*) unless I had telescopic arms and then I'd look stupid . . . You two can stop laughing as well unless you want a bit of that.

DON You carry on with your cleaning, Mr Sheen.

JIM I always knew you were a scrubber, Nod.

Jim and Don laugh whilst Noddy scrubs more and more furiously.

NODDY (*throwing his rag down and rolling up his sleeves in preparation for a fight*) Right, that does it!

DAVE (*reappearing at door with two steaming mugs of Cup-A-Soup*) Right, I've had just about enough of you, Neville, get up to your room . . .

NODDY But those two . . .

DAVE Now!

At this point Ozzy Osbourne enters the room.

EVERYONE All right, Ozzy.

OZZY

OZZY All right, Slade . . . Sorry to interrupt your dinner but I think I left a glass of Tizer here this afternoon . . . Has anyone seen it? I'm parched.

NODDY You what?

Noddy headbutts Ozzy and he falls to the ground. The rest of Slade gather round Noddy and point at him in a comical manner. Close-up of Noddy and the pointing happy group members as Noddy lets out the following cry:

NODDY Get down and get with it!

The perfick
The Midget Gem
The Boston Strangler
The Cry of the Walnut
The Plop Festival
The Emma Peel
The Passage to India
The Hushed Puppy
The Juniper Conspiracy
The Angel's Delight
The Faberge Egg

THE CARDINAL'S ERROR

of Jean De Florette II

The Operation Poodle
The Mouse that roared
The Lemon Pipe

THE EMMA PEEL &
A TREBLE HOT WINNIE

The Foreign Foghorn
The Shepherd's Crook
The Todd Carty

The Sweet William
The Cardinal's
    Error

The Ipcress File
The Little Man
The Stealer
The Pillion passenger
The Gino Ginelli

THE FABERGE EGG &

The Hot Winnie
The Cockerel Cometh
The Whistling Broom Handle
&
THE SWEET WILLIAM (BILL)

Can
U
SPOT
'EM?

21

BRITISH INFORMATION BOARD
– THE COUNTRY CODE

NB *This section is a filmed piece which basically shows our two comic actors larking about in the countryside breaking the rules of the Country Code. It should have the feel of a mid-70s industrial information film, i.e. KPM jaunty library music, very bright Eastman colour. If possible a cold sunny winter's day to give a slightly sad and sinister feel. Camerawork should be highly factual rather than fancy.*

Voice-over by Patrick Allen

Many, many years ago it seemed perfectly natural for young fit men to greet each other in wooded areas and play awhile to pass the time. Nowadays, it seems that young men are forced to meet behind closed doors for clandestine candlelit dinners for two in the Garrick Club. Hmmm hmmm. So, OK, times change so what was once a simple display of affection is now seen as a revolting and vulgar perversion. Who are we to say . . . At this point Rick Parfitt again strode arrogantly into our office, grabbed the typewriter and hurled it violently into the crowded bazaar in the street below. Ownership of the typewriter changed hands several times in the space of a few minutes and it was eventually recovered in exchange for 18 clay hats.

Titles

A light green screen. The words 'British Information Board' giving the overall and undeniable impression of a title sequence. Switch to picture of a haystack over which are the words 'The Country Code'. Switch to still of Vic and Bob in their Graham Hill garments over which are the words 'featuring Jack Dent & Eric Potter'.

In this piece Vic and Bob are dressed like Graham Hill the fast car driver, i.e. checked flat cap, checked tweed sports jackets, 1 × white shirt and club tie, 1 × yellow polo neck, 2 × black flannel slacks and their own shoes, you know just whatever they turn up in, and 2 × brown leather kid gloves. They both have Graham Hill moustaches, slightly thickened eyebrows and additional earhair.

Scene One

Camera pans a nice area of countryside and focuses in on Vic and Bob who are busy wallpapering a plough in a field.

VOICE-OVER *(very authoritative voice, e.g. Patrick Allen)* Hey, you.

Vic and Bob turn to camera.

VIC & BOB Who . . . us?

VOICE-OVER Yes, you.

VIC & BOB What?

VOICE-OVER Have you just wallpapered that plough?

VIC & BOB *(with a 'what business is it of yours' look)* Yes.

VOICE-OVER Are you aware that the wallpapering of ploughs is prohibited under the Country Code?

VIC & BOB No.

VOICE-OVER Well it is. For it can cause plowright distraction leading to seed misplacement.

Vic and Bob look sheepish and mouth the word 'sorry'.

CUT TO

SHEEP VIBRATING PLATFORM

CHUGGA CHUGGA

HULL 40m

Scene Two

Again we pan across countryside to focus in upon Vic and Bob who are standing next to a sheep that is being vibrated upon a flat steel platform similar to a railway station luggage weighing machine. They are standing idly smoking cigarettes as if they were waiting for their lunchbreak to end.

VOICE-OVER Hey, you.

VIC & BOB What us?

VOICE-OVER Is that your sheep?

VIC & BOB No.

VOICE-OVER Are you aware that sheep vibrating is prohibited under the Country Code?

VIC & BOB No.

VOICE-OVER Well it is. For it can cause wool entanglement leading to misshapen cardy.

VIC & BOB Sorry.

Scene Three

Zoom in to reveal our comedy actors pumping cavity wall insulation foam directly into a beautiful dry stone wall. An ideal dry stone wall is located just past the Stag Inn in Reeth, North Yorkshire. Take the A1 or M1 to Scotch Corner. Then take the A174 to Richmond, North Yorkshire (if you have time stop off there and admire the historic castle, market square and Green Howards Museum. If military history is not your cup of tea then how about a real cup of tea and perhaps a light snack (ham) at the castle tea-rooms that are situated next to the castle car park).

From Richmond, North Yorkshire take the B1127 to Reeth, North Yorkshire. If you have the time why not stop off at one of the many picnic areas situated along the beautiful primrose-lined banks of the River Swale, North Yorkshire. Incidentally, you are now deep within Herriot Country and may wish to visit one of the locations used for the popular Sunday evening comedy programme about a hapless vet and his overbearing senior partner, alcoholic womanizing, younger brother and repeatedly reincarnating, accident prone, buxom, pie-cooking white witch of a wife.

The Stag Inn is situated on the corner of the Hawes and Barnard Castle, North Yorkshire crossroads. Park your car in the pub car park and if you have time why not pop into the pub and sample one of the delicious lagers that are stocked, e.g. Carling Black Label, Castlemaine, and Tennents Super Extra lager.

There is also a large selection of bar meals available at competitive prices including:

MENU

Starters		Main course	
Biscuits	80p	Ham in wine	£14.99
Pan boiled tomatoes	40p	Dime bar in new fat	£8.74
Fat	£1.80	Shallow fried grouse:	
Top of the milk	25p	whole	£22.50
Ricicles	30p	half	£22.46

The above are served with a choice of Thick Sauce, Thin Sauce, Juice, button mushrooms, crisps and a whole roast chicken.

Puddings		Beverages (drinks)	
Frozen top of the milk	26p	Top of the milk	24p
Hand varnished pears	72p	Orange squash	10p
Whelks in hot tap		Wine drink:	
water	£1.00	bottle	£2.40
Hot vinegar cup	5p	per cup	80p

All orders to be placed at the bar.

The actual wall can be found by following the public footpath to Arthgarthensdale which is to the side of the pub. The wall is approximately 800 yards along the path.

If travelling by air take British Midlands flight BM132 from Heathrow to Teesside airport and take one of the numerous airport taxis to Scotch Corner or hire a car from the Hertz outlet at the airport where British Midland travellers can obtain specially discounted rates (unlike bloody Avis who don't seem to bother with discounts, well, not that we're aware of anyway).

Scene Three Continued

VOICE-OVER   Hey, you.

VIC & BOB   Who us?

VOICE-OVER   Yes, you. Is that your cavity wall insulation unit?

VIC & BOB   No . . . why?

VOICE-OVER   Never mind why, now clear off.

VIC & BOB   *(disappointedly and slightly annoyed)* Oh you can't do 'owt round here. *(Vic and Bob throw down foam injection pipes in disgust.)*

Scene Four

Vic and Bob are stood in a clearing in a woodland glade. One of them is leaning against a tree. They are having a nice little chat and there might well be a little bit of giggling.

VOICE-OVER   Hey, you.

VIC & BOB   What now?

VOICE-OVER   Are you wearing lipstick?

VIC & BOB   Yes *(in an 'is it really any of your business' manner).*

VOICE-OVER   It's very nice . . . What colour is it?

VIC   *(to Bob)* It's Peach Supper, isn't it?

BOB   No, I think it's Peach Party . . . Hold on, what's it got to do with you?

VIC   Yeah, you nosey parker . . . you want to take a look at yourself in the mirror . . . you're nowt but a spring onion.

Camera immediately switches to a man dressed in a red Spandex cat suit, white cowboy boots, white silk shirt, red leather jacket with large shoulder pads and elaborate cobweb embroidery. He is holding a blue electric guitar. He has a small 30-watt combo amp. His head is that of a spring onion (see drawing).

SPRING ONION   *(with Tommy Vance voice)* I know I am but that's not going to stop me rocking. *(Spring Onion Man strikes his guitar and we hear some heavy metal chords ring out across the forest.)*

Zoom in to close-up of Spring Onion's face as he unleashes a primal scream. His mouth is distorted and misshapen. His cry gradually permeates the forest as might the cry of Sasquatch on learning that his wife has mistakenly seasoned the potatoes with Harpic again.

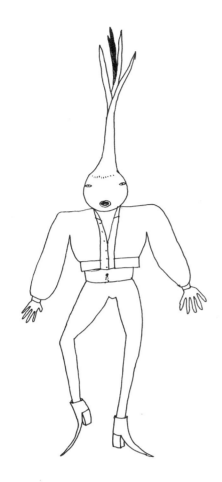

SPRING ONION

CUT TO   Still of Jack and Eric's faces, this time clearly with lipstick adorning their lips and mascara and blue eyeshadow enhancing their beautiful eyes.

Over this image the following titles are run:

A British Information Board Presentation

(large B.I.B. logo)

Jack Dent & Eric Potter
are currently appearing in
'Hands Off That's My Hearing Aid'
at Hull Town Hall, Hull

VOICE-OVER   *(female)* The British Information Board is funded by Revlon Cosmetics Limited.

CELEBRITY GUEST: LOVEJOY

VIC   And now, ladies and gentlemen, let me introduce you to this week's celebrity guest . . . you'll know him as the lovable rogue who readily exercises rights of access and passage to country homes owned by elderly widows. Please welcome . . . Lovejoy.

Enter Lovejoy (Bob). (See drawing.)

VIC   Thank you for coming . . . Now, everybody knows you as Lovejoy but presumably you have a first name . . . What is it might I ask?

LOVE   *(using the voice of a Red Indian chief)* Joy Nktonga.

VIC   That's a very nice name . . . Now, Lovejoy, the scenery and the locations you use are always very beautiful . . . Where exactly is it filmed?

LOVE   On the plains of Calamyer. Beyond the forest of the spirits, across the lake with boat hire and beneath the volcano our forefathers named Sleeping Brute.

VIC   That's a nice name . . . for a volcano . . . now when did you first get interested in antique stroke detective work?

LOVE   No, like the male perfume Brut.

VIC   Oh right . . . Roll on or atomizer?

LOVE   Me not know . . . Brut is old fashioned. Now in village we use Paco Raban.

VIC   What a nice name for a perfume . . . Now, when did you first get interested in antique stroke detective work?

LOVE   I was young. My father take me to edge of the great plain. I see many people below me *(sweeping arm movement)*, many have air guns, some have gatties and a few have the long bendy stick for shitty shotty.

SELLOTAPE FOR EYE 'POUCHES'

TIGHT WHITE 'T' SHIRT

BROWN LEATHER 'BOMBER' JACKET

TIGHT 'BLUE' JEANS

'COW'BOY BOOTS

LOVE JOY

VIC Oh that's a nice name for a weapon. Then what happened?

LOVE Later me and family go on holiday to Inverness . . . It's a lovely place . . . do you know it?

VIC No, but it's a nice name for a holiday resort.

LOVE For three days and three nights I watch *Man From Uncle* . . . Then the rains stop and my father he teach me the ways of his father and his father before him and we go oggy raiding.

VIC What's that?

LOVE Stealing apples.

VIC Oh, isn't that a nice name for apple theft.

LOVE Anyway I climb orchard wall and see below me many people guarding the oggy. Some with air gun, some with gatty and a few with the bendy stick for shitty shotty . . .

Love turns to camera to deliver one of the famous asides that he has become keen on. He uses Bob's real voice (if you can call that high-pitched whine a voice in the first place). Hey, hang on, that would be a good name for a fish restaurant as would any of the following:

Oh My Cod	*Shaddup You Dace*
Eel by Gum	*Hail Me a Crab*
The John Dory Story	*The Shrimpsons*
Timmy Mullets	*On Yer Pike*
Fish You Were Here	*The Frying Doctors*
Fishing On a Star	*Do They Mean Huss?*
Chips My Party	*Captain Ballpoint*

At this point Mike Yarwood entered the office brandishing the original designs for that split second between dawn and dusk belonging to Sir Charles Greaves who, unbeknown to us, had been relaxing under our desk all afternoon wearing a satin slip and drawing tiny pictures of monkeys' ears on our legs. Mike announced that he had been sleeping with Sir Charles's wife and had stolen the drawings from the incubator in which Sir Charles is breeding miniature penguins. (To be continued.)

LOVE Hey, now remember, be careful if handling any of these weapons because all of them could potentially take one of your eyes out *(leans over to Vic and points slowly at each of his eyes in turn)*. Either that one . . . or that one.

VIC Orchard's a nice name for an enclosed area of fruit-bearing trees. But, Lovejoy *(short period of over and under circular hand groilling)*, how did this all lead to your interest in antiques?

LOVE I climb down from wall and for two hours and forty days I eat Chewies. I grow angry and fire grenade from my Johnny Seven, but spring proves defective and grenade veers to the east knocking Stretch Armstrong off the tree . . . Armstrong fall on to Matchbox motorized motorway causing pile up . . . I seek forgiveness and ride for many miles over the mountains in my Spiderman outfit but this was no ordinary journey for my bike was without stabilizers and so I come to be here.

VIC Fascinating . . . thank you very much, Lovejoy, it's been wonderful.

SONG: 'LET'S HAVE A LOOK AT IT'

I love the smell of manure,
I love the smell of the poor,
I love the smell of Frank Muir.

Chorus
So come on now, let's have a look at it,
Come on now, let's have a sniff of it,
Come on, Bob, let's look a little bit more.

I love the smell of a flannel,
I love the smell of an old oak panel,
I love the smell of the hair of a spaniel.

Chorus
I love the smell of mixed grill,
I love the smell of Vince Hill,
I love the smell of Spender's espadrilles.

Chorus
I love the smell of Kung Fu,
I love the smell of Whipsnade Zoo,
I love the smell of Lulu's hairdo.

Chorus

NB *During the above song:*

a. Vic and Bob Hold up items from the pile of stuff to illustrate each smell.

b. In the two bars following the second chorus, Vic bends to pick up an item with his arse near Bob's face. A squealing farting sound is heard. Vic rises . . . He is clutching a child's squeaky toy.

CLOSING TITLES

VICTORIAN STRAWBERRY DREAM SEQUENCE

CUT TO   Victorian strawberry dream sequence.

Via wavy dream sequence wipe.

London 1890, a hansom cab draws up on cobbles outside a residential door. It is night with a slight fog. A mysterious figure alights wearing topper and cloak. He raps on the door with his cane. The door is opened by a Bruce Forsyth lookalike.

BRUCE   Dibdibdibdibdib, nice to see you, to see you nice, dibdibdib, not nice, ah, dib dib dibdib,

if you want to bet on it then you better get on it a du du du du. Let's have a look at the board, Miss Ford.

Midway through this dialogue, camera pulls back and dark figure turns to face it, revealing that his head is a strawberry.

An aston flashes up in a star at the bottom right-hand side of the screen with the title 'strawberry' in it. £4.99

KING

DIB DIB DIB !! NOT NICE NOT NICE YOU DONT GET NUFFINK FER A PEAR NO, NO! NOT IN VIS GAME. WHAT! NO NO GUV!

BRUCE FORSYTHE (GENERATION GAME)

SHOW

Alan,

enclosed is script N° 2

I hope you like it.

Jim & Bob x

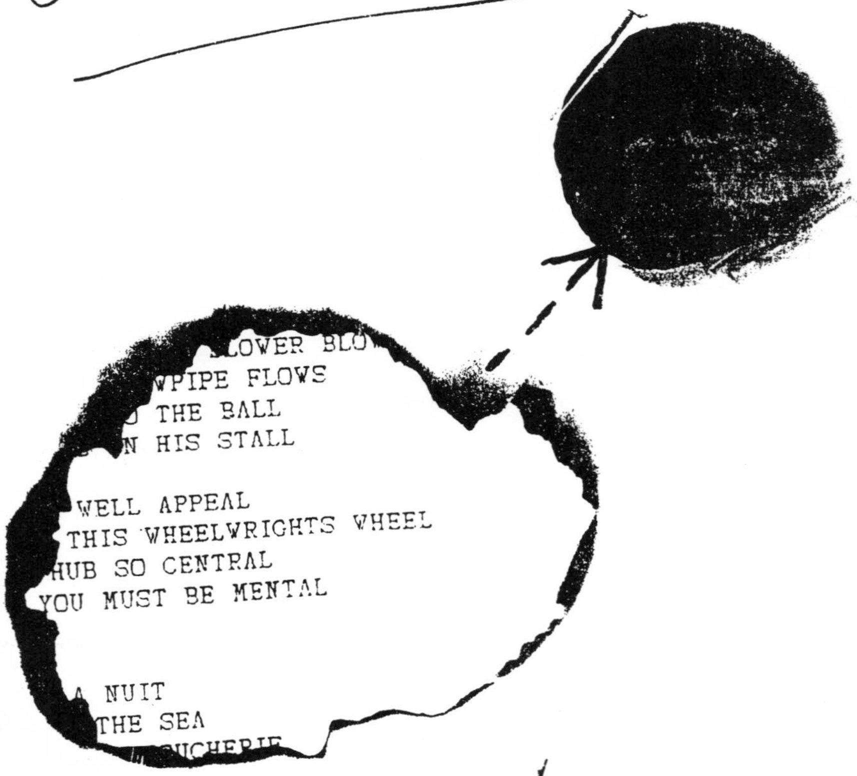

```
     LOWER BLO
   WPIPE FLOWS
   THE BALL
  N HIS STALL

   WELL APPEAL
    THIS WHEELWRIGHTS WHEEL
  HUB SO CENTRAL
  YOU MUST BE MENTAL

   A NUIT
   THE SEA
    UCHERIE
```

WOW!

(the power of
the dried apricot)

NB This show is a 'milk pan special' — pans may be attached to clothing, hair, vans, etc. at any given moment.

OPENING TITLES

Yarn *(Voice-over by Patrick Allen)*

In '18 Nickingten 8' German plumber Gerhart Brugel invents the liquid we now know as water. In 1927 fellow countryman Rolph Müller invents the tap, but failing to see the potential of his invention simply marketed it as a dishcloth holder cum plug tidy. Within weeks he is bankrupt and his invention lies dormant until 1967 when American forces sweetheart Glen Cooper had the bright idea of combining the two. Since that date, literally thousands of gallons of water have been pumped directly into people's homes, filling cups and mugs, kettles and jugs, pots, pans and, for special occasions, this commemorative glass goblet.

Ladies and gentlemen, please welcome the makers of that beautiful goblet . . . Reeves and Mortimer.

Camera pulls back from the very heart of a glassblowers' ball. The first shot is beautiful beyond the beauty of even the youngest shrimp in the deep blue waters of the North Atlantic. Fire, yes, fire seems to consume the camera lens as it licks the glassblower's ball in a circular manner. The camera pulls back gradually revealing the glassblower's magnificent rod and onward to reveal the puffing cheeks of the glassblower himself . . . Elton Kent.

Camera pulls back further to reveal Vic gazing upon this fiery scene. Vic is reading a book entitled Inside Information – The Secrets of the Glassblower's Trade *by Lonnie Donegan. He is fascinated by both the blower and the*

information *within the book (as anyone would be if they took the time to study this fascinating craft).*

Vic commences singing the operetta Le pain de la mer dans la nuit *(The Seabread of the Night).*

Bob, for his crimes, is standing gazing wistfully admiring a working wheelwright who interestingly was born during the General Strike in 1926.

Also arranged around the set at their work are a wedding photographer, a dry cleaner, a cavity wall insulator and the singer out of Go West (Irish pop group). As Vic and Bob introduce these craftsmen to the audience they sing the haunting operetta.

VIC The glass ball glows as the glassblower blows
a tiny glass swan from his blowpipe flows,
a hot narrow wind blasts into the ball,
producing these goods here on his stall.

BOB Those delicate swans may well appeal,
but come take a look at this wheelwright's wheel,
the rim, the spokes, the hub so central,
to prefer glass swans you must be mental.

Chorus
Le pain de la mer dans la nuit,
The sweet sweet bread of the sea,
Les grand garçons est dans la boucherie,
The big boys are in the butcher's.

VIC The dirt leaves the scene as the dry cleaner cleans,
some sick out of a hat and some blood-encrusted jeans.
Your wheel is quite round that I doubt not,
but my dry cleaning drum is both round . . . and quite hot.

VIC I'm beautifully dressed.

BLOKE OUT OF GO WEST

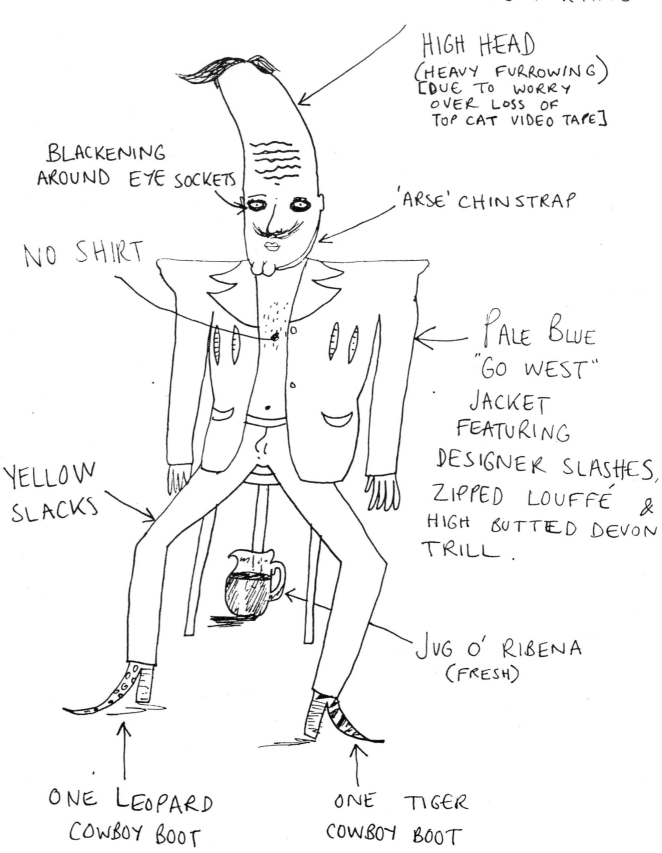

18" SIDE PARTING

HIGH HEAD
(HEAVY FURROWING)
[DUE TO WORRY
OVER LOSS OF
TOP CAT VIDEO TAPE]

BLACKENING
AROUND EYE SOCKETS

'ARSE' CHINSTRAP

NO SHIRT

PALE BLUE
"GO WEST"
JACKET
FEATURING
DESIGNER SLASHES,
ZIPPED LOUFFÉ &
HIGH BUTTED DEVON
TRILL.

YELLOW
SLACKS

JUG O' RIBENA
(FRESH)

ONE LEOPARD
COWBOY BOOT

ONE TIGER
COWBOY BOOT

BOB You're cleaner obsessed
And you've not impressed the bloke from
Go West.

VIC But what does he do?

BOB I'll show you, you fool,
He hides Ribena under his stool.

Chorus (with an unseen choir of children)

VIC & BOB

Vic and Bob then introduce themselves to each other and the audience and make their way to the desk. As they do so the various craftsmen shuffle off stage except for the singer out of Go West (see drawing) who remains seated in his original position.

When seated Vic and Bob pursue the following 'quickfire' jokes.

BOB Before we start can you clear something up for me, Vic?

VIC Yes, go on.

BOB Thanks (*pouring curtain hooks on to the desk*).

VIC That's very funny (*sarcastically*). Achoo (*i.e. a sneeze*).

BOB Bless you.

VIC No, I've just noticed that picture of a Jew on the desk. (*Points to framed picture of rabbi on desk – or a picture of a shoe.*)

BOB That's very, very funny. I watched *My Left Foot* last night.

VIC Oh, with Daniel Day Lewis?

BOB No, just me and the wife.

VIC That's very funny that.

And so on and so on. Following the last of the above traditional jokes we again see alternate close-ups on Vic and Bob laughing hysterically as in Show 1.

VIC Well later on we've got a McVicar lookalike who's going to smear essence of Colette all over a sitar previously owned by Labi Siffre's Hairnet Keeper . . . Now that's interesting because Labi Siffre was a very hairy man . . .

As Vic continues to carp on about Labi's back and leg hair, Bob picks up the harpoon from the side of the desk in a bored yet slightly inquisitive manner (as one might do if one chanced across some mouse droppings in a naval officer's sink). Suddenly the harpoon goes off propelling Bob violently out of frame like so many mouse droppings being hurled from a naval officer's bucket against the back wall of a drunken foghorn operator's pathetic hovel . . .

VIC He would backcomb all his back and neck hair into a nice horn and hang up his hat or his duffle bag with his lunchbox in it . . . usually a nice bit of cheese and an Opal Fruit. And he'd put his arm hair into a nice sort of hair curtain and open it up for the ladies to display a little peanut wearing a pair of cycling shorts . . .

At around this point Bob returns to his seat. He has suffered the following bizarre injuries (see drawing).

1. He has a cotton-wool milking stool on his head
2. He has had his right eyebrow thickened to one inch
3. His upper lip has been customized by use of hot dry wind leading to undercurl
4. Prince's (the pop singer's) tiny milk pan has become attached to his cheek

VIC (*suddenly noticing Bob's return and his terrible injuries*) Where have you been? What's all that muck on your face?

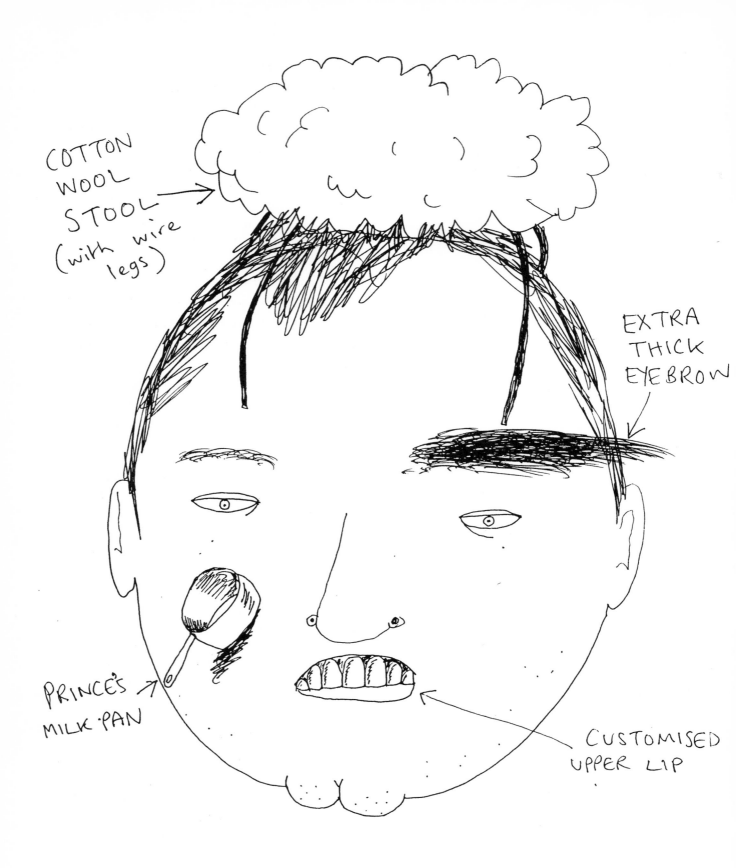

COTTON WOOL STOOL (with wire legs)

EXTRA THICK EYEBROW

PRINCE'S MILK PAN

CUSTOMISED UPPER LIP

BOB'S INJURIES

BOB   Just leave it, will you.

VIC   Hold on, I've seen injuries like that before.

BOB   Just leave it.

VIC   Now where was it? . . . It was exactly the same injuries . . . Hold on, let me have a look in me book . . . (Vic picks up book from the desk entitled I Spy Terrible Injuries. He begins to flick through the pages of the book in the manner that a bank clerk would rifle through a wad of notes and alternately licking his fingers very rapidly. NB These 'finger' shots are in extreme close-up and are rapidly interchanged with each other and also close-up shots of Bob's staring face.)

Overall the above scene should give the impression of an assistant manager of a Dixon's electrical supply shop (soon to become actual manager), trying to alert his manager (soon to be laid off due to his involvement with an attaché case), to a swan with its beak caught in a lemon crusher.

VIC   Aah, I think I've got it . . . Bob, can you say, Shaftesbury Avenue?

BOB   'Course I can. Shedsferew Aahhbrew Aahbrew!

VIC   Yes, thought as much. You've been projected through the air by harpoon, dragged through an eyebrow thickening booth, forced to work in an upper lip customizing clinic and made to boil up Prince's milk for his tea. Now inevitably this has led to Shaftesbury Avenue memory loss (pointing to cotton wool milking stool on Bob's head). Come on, Bob, fight it. Shaftesbury Avenue, Shaftesbury Avenue, Shaftesbury Avenue.

Close-up of Vic's face chanting the above . . . Wavy dream wipe . . . Shaftesbury Avenue Dream.

CUT TO   Pre-recorded insert as follows: camera is looking down from the gallery of a Victorian lecture theatre where a patient is having his bandages removed from his very round head by a surgeon and his nurse. An aston on the screen reads, 'Shaftesbury Avenue, 1909'.

The camera swoops down to the bandage removal. The camera must not show either the surgeon's or the patient's faces. Cut to the Victorian audience as they gasp as the last piece of bandage is removed. Cut back to the nurse staring at the patient with a shocked expression. Then cut to patient. He is a beautiful blonde Victorian male with a waxed moustache and a monocle. He puts an already lit pipe into his mouth and rises from his seat to thank the surgeon. As they shake hands the surgeon turns round to camera to reveal that he is in fact . . . an onion.

The audience throw up their hats in celebration shouting 'God bless the onion, thank God for the onion, etc., etc.'

CUT TO   Coming out of dreamy wipe and back to Bob who is now cured and is chanting 'Shaftesbury Avenue'. Vic congratulates Bob on his recovery (and indeed why shouldn't he be congratulated?).

UNCLE PETER AND THE SINGER FROM GO WEST

Bob and Vic ponce over to where Peter and the singer are situated.

PETER   Go West. You're not needed.

SINGER   Whooaaggh.

Bob and Vic silence the singer and ask Peter what the problem is here.

PETER He won't go, fellows. I've given it me best, but he won't go.

BOB Why not, Pete?

PETER Apparently someone has stolen his Top Cat video cassette.

SINGER Whooaaggh.

VIC That's awful, I know how you feel. I lost a very dear relative recently.

BOB You told me it was a very dear wristwatch you lost.

VIC Well, yeah, me uncle was wearing it when he was shot.

BOB Anyway that's not half as bad as this fellow's loss.

VIC I tell you what, Bob, let's see if Otis and Marvin can help.

CUT TO

OTIS AND MARVIN

Pre-recorded insert of Otis Redding and Marvin Gaye on a dockside wall.

BOB Otis, can you help this man? He's had his Top Cat video cassette stolen.

OTIS Well, first off, Bob, I'd like to say how very sorry I am to hear about the young boy's terrible loss . . . but it's not an uncommon problem to use an animated character such as Top Cat or Sylvester or Felix . . .

MARVIN Well, any of the animated cats really, Otis.

OTIS Yes . . . To use them as a focus for problems you're having elsewhere, for instance at school . . .

MARVIN Yes, this young man is obviously being bullied at school . . . Now, there are a few practical things he should do immediately. Firstly, he should stop taking his dinner money to school and instead take a packed lunch.

OTIS But be careful not to take stuff in your box that might entice a bully like Wotsits, Camembert, jugged hare.

MARVIN But, most importantly, you've got to realize that you've reached the stage in your life where you are going through certain changes.

OTIS Yes, you will notice that your voice is changing, the shape of your body is altering; because you're turning into a beautiful young woman.

MARVIN Yes, a very beautiful young woman.

OTIS But this isn't the only change you can expect. No, in a further four years' time you will turn into a bear.

MARVIN Yes, a very beautiful brown bear and then seven years hence you will sprout wings and become a beautiful seagull.

OTIS Yes a very beautiful and wise gull . . . Sorry, Bob . . . What was your original question?

BOB We just wondered if you could help this singer get over the theft of his Top Cat video.

OTIS Oh, that's easy. Uncle Pete's got the video in his pocket.

VIC What! Peter, is this true?

PETER Yes *(handing over video to singer)*. Don't send me back.

BOB Why, Peter, why?

PETER I just wanted to see what a cat looks like . . . I didn't want to hurt him . . . Don't send me back . . .

VIC   Peter, you should have said . . . *(taking video back off pop singer and inserting it into a video machine)* Here . . . watch it . . . You don't mind do you, love?

CUT TO   Video screen. Initially the screen is showing a clip from an episode of Top Cat.

NB The dialogue for the above clip will be provided by Vic and Bob and with a touch of good fortune will be quite amusing. In fact it might just pull this sketch out of the quagmire into which it is being inextricably yet inevitably drawn very much as a sabre-toothed tiger was once drawn to the whimper of a young deer as it struggled to free itself from the grip of the tar within the tar pits, La Brae tar pits, 1120 Wiltshire/Santa Monica. Los Angeles USA.*

Suddenly and amateurishly the cartoon changes to a home video of the Uncle Peter Band performing the following song:

PETER   I want to kill a fly,
But I haven't got the time.

I'll get an expert in
To shoot the bloody thing/swine

BOB & VIC   Yes, Peter, yes, that's what you
should do
And while the experts are here
We'll have him shoot some deer.
(or)
Yes, Peter, yes, that's what you
should do
and when the fly is gone
we'll go and kill that swan.
(or)

Yes, Peter, yes, that's what you
should do
(spoken) But get a couple of
estimates first.

We pull back from the video screen.

VIC   Peter, you've taped over his Top Cat cartoon.

PETER   Will I have to go back to the dark place?

BOB   Yes, Peter, we're going to have to report this incident to the Silvikrin Foundation for hair fruiting . . .

Interrupted by pop singer who by now is understandably languishing in a bath of hen juice mending a pre-war wireless and singeing a young mouse's snout whiskers with one of them disposable lighters with a woman on the side whose dress comes down when the lighter is inverted.

NB The speech below is simply mouthed out of sync to pre-recorded video.

SINGER   Now just hold it right there. Now I thoroughly enjoyed that sampler of the Uncle Peter Band and it has exorcized from my mind all that pish posh about animated cats. You know, I don't mind if I never see a talking cat again. I'd like to hear some more of the Uncle Peter Band and, in fact, I think that song is going to put Go West right back in the charts where they belong . . . Uncle Peter, come and meet my manager Bruin the Bear.

Exit Peter and pop singer with Bob and Vic left dumbfounded.

---

* For more information on the fascinating subject of tar grip please write to Professor José San Carlos at UCLA University, Tar Department, Louis Grandos Building, 1130 Sunset/Ventura, Los Angeles CA, USA.

PAT ☆ 🍒 DAVE ☆ ♡

UH UH

SASSY!

ULT

Pat Wright & Dave Arrowsmith.

Pat & Dave met on the set of the BBC Drama The Lotus Eaters when they were running ~~rival~~ catering services: Actorfeed and Steven Spielburger

DAVE FAX

DAVE IS CUTE

DAVE IS RICH!! RICH! RICH!!

DAVE IS SOOOO EROTIC SASSY!

PAT DAVE

PAT

PATÉ

PATER PATERNOSTER

DAVE Davy

PATHE NEWS

PATTI SMITH

THE BRA MEN AT THE PAPER SHOP

Dave and Pat

Vic and Bob, dressed in donkey jackets, enter a bog standard, small, corner shop newsagents. The newsagent is a timid, slim, forty-year-old wearing a grey, V-neck sweater, a green checked shirt and a red woollen tie. He has a pen in the crux of his 'V'. On his right breast is a season-ticket-sized identification photocard with the name 'Ray' on it. The photograph shows Ray's head which has been terribly startled in the photobooth by a zombie with its tits on fire.

DAVE (VIC)   All right, mate . . . now Pat here wants a birthday card for his nephew . . . Isn't that right, Pat?

PAT (BOB)   Aye.

DAVE   Now he's a young lad of twelve, he likes football and trains . . . Isn't that right, Pat?

PAT   Aye.

DAVE   Now have you got owt?

SHOP OWNER   *(turning to card display behind him and lifting a card that features a vase of flowers and the words 'Grandma' in gold lettering)* Let's see what we've got.

DAVE   *(quickly interjecting)* Aye, that will do.

SHOP OWNER   But this is for Grandma.

Close-up shot of shopkeeper's finger pointing to the word Grandma.

CUT TO   Full-length shot of shopkeeper pointing to card alone in centre of shop.

CUT TO   Shot of Pat and Dave staring inquisitively at the card in order to try and work out why it is apparently the wrong card.

CUT TO   Original 3 shot.

PAT   It's all right, that . . . wrap it up.

Shopkeeper commences placing card in paper bag whilst shaking his head and unveiling a light, ironic, twittering laugh.

DAVE   Ow, mate, what's your problem, mate? . . . Something funny like?

SHOPKEEPER   *(meekly)* No, not at all.

PAT   You laughing at our bras?

DAVE   Something funny about us wearing bras?

PAT   Yeah, you got a problem with that, mate . . . do you want to make something of it?

SHOPKEEPER   No, no, not at all . . . I'm sorry.

DAVE   You will be sorry, mate . . . I hate your type. It's all just a big joke to you, isn't it?

PAT   Come on, Dave. You can keep your bloody card *(starts exiting)*, not going to stay here and be insulted by you.

Leaves with card in hand.

CUT TO   Exterior of shop. Dave has just shut the door.

PAT   Hey, Dave, I didn't say owt like, but I'm not wearing me bra today.

DAVE   You mean I caused that fuss for nowt . . .

PAT   I know, Dave man, but I didn't want him thinking I wasn't wearing one, you know.

Dave and Pat walk off along the street. About ten yards on, they cross paths with a smartly dressed 26-year-old woman. As they cross, Dave and Pat confront her with the following speech which is heard as it were slightly in the distance.

DAVE   You laughing at our bras?

PAT   You got a problem with it like?

ANTIQUES ROADSHOW

All of a sudden Vic adopts a head pose where his head is thrust forwards and upwards to achieve a protruding chin. He is mouthing in the way a goldfish might if it were starved of oxygen and placed on some rough sandpaper. He is making the noise an old man (e.g. Mr Rodgers, 73 years) might make if gently punched in the stomach.

VIC   Bob, have you seen my choker?

Camera then goes into extreme close-up of a choker on Vic's neck that has been drawn on to the neck skin using a uniball x 3 quadrant deluxe felt pen. A finger then comes into shot and starts to scratch the choker. An overly loud sound effect accompanies the finger movement.

Camera pulls back to reveal Bob standing in one of the most ridiculous stances one could imagine still scratching the choker on Vic's neck.

VIC   How much do you reckon it's worth?

BOB   Haven't a clue, Vic, it looks like an antique to me.

VIC   Well spotted, Bob, that's why I had it valued (turning to camera) at the Antiques Roadshow.

CUT TO   Titles for Antiques Roadshow: still photograph of a modern brass carriage clock that is being lightly tapped by a fish slice; at the top, the words 'Antiques Roadshow'; at the bottom, 'presented by Hugh Skully' (or A Huge Skullery or A Huge Skull). First image is a close-up of a felt pen choker being scratched (as above).

Camera pulls back to reveal a middle-aged man sat at a table holding his neck out for choker inspection. The choker is being scratched by an 'expert' in a three-piece suit. The table they are sat at has a sign on it saying 'Chokers'.

There is a queue of five further middle-aged men waiting to have their chokers inspected and all adopting the choker inspection pose.

The expert is nodding his head and intermittently playing 'air trumpet'.

Camera pulls back further to reveal in the foreground Hugh Skully and in the background all the activity we associate with the Antiques Roadshow . . . You know the kind of thing . . . brass.

Hugh Skully (see drawing) (Bob) has ink castellations on frontis headline, he is wearing a pair of black headphones with high supporting stirrups incorporating a brass bell. He has distinct black worry lines which deepen with every appearance as he gets into deeper trouble. He has a single 'chappaquiddick'. He has a stuffed monkey on one shoulder and another on his waist (by the end of sketch he has four monkeys attached to his person).

HUGH   Chokers proving very popular here at the Dennis Norden Murray Mint Memorial Hall in Canterbury Cathedral, York Minster . . . Wait for it! . . . Coventry.

The crowd cheers hurrah! as anyone would do on hearing their hometown mentioned on television.

CUT TO   VT of various 47-year-olds clapping and whooping, all filmed in an unusual and varied way. Perhaps the screen could be split to give the impression of a Victorian prostitute fiddling in her purse to find a pair of brass tweezers previously owned by the little sex-mad old woman out of The Crankies.

HUGH   (the cheering having abruptly stopped) First off, let's join Johnny 'Parrot Face' Baldwin and see what he's got.

Johnny is sat at a table examining the foreleg of a greyhound. He is speaking to a 57-year-old middle-class woman with a maroon wool suit and a lovely Liberty shawl over her shoulders. This shawl could possibly steal the show as it's a top of the range one with privet leaves and handcuffs

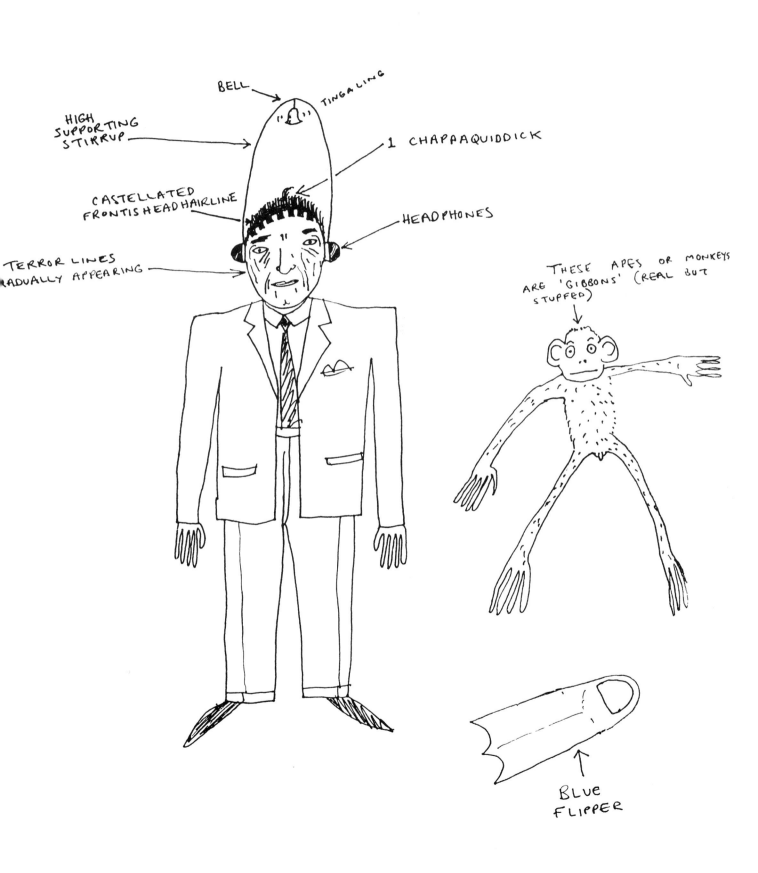

BELL

TINGALING

HIGH
SUPPORTING
STIRRUP

1 CHAPPAQUIDDICK

CASTELLATED
FRONTISHEAD HAIRLINE

HEADPHONES

TERROR LINES
GRADUALLY APPEARING

THESE APES OR MONKEYS
ARE 'GIBBONS' (REAL BUT
STUFFED)

BLUE
FLIPPER

printed all over it in gold with a red background and blue border . . . It must have cost a fortune, certainly significantly more than say a Hermes and they cost an arm and a leg, mind you all you get with a Hermes is a print of a dozy penguin or a horse or something like that. It makes you think, doesn't it?

Huddled around the table in the usual roadshow manner are typical roadshow punters. They have brought with them items such as: 2-litre tub of cheap margarine; branch with Xmas baubles on it; a great big 'postmen don't bend' birthday card with a soppy elephant on the front; an inflatable dinosaur.

JOHNNY   Yes, it's quite unusual as the toenails are still intact. Let's have a look at the back and see what that reveals. Aaah yes, well, it's definitely a greyhound.

LADY   Yes.

JOHNNY   It's a male.

LADY   Yes.

JOHNNY   It's one of four.

LADY   Yes.

JOHNNY   The weft of the pelt means it's probably this century.

LADY   Yes.

JOHNNY   But interestingly there is a suspended rear foot Norton.

LADY   Yes.

JOHNNY   Which would suggest nineteenth century, as dogs stopped having them around 1870, 1875 as a mark of respect for Queen Victoria's death.

LADY   Yes.

NB *During the above all the people in the hall gradually join in with the ladies 'Yes', this is just heard until the final 'Yes' when camera shows that the people queuing at the table are all saying 'Yes' in sync with the lady.*

JOHNNY   You don't happen to know what the dog was called, do you?

LADY   Yes, Parrot Face, he was called 'Barkie'.

JOHNNY   Oh, Barkie, my goodness, well that's wonderful . . . Pieces of Barkie have been fetching fantastic prices at auction recently . . . You don't happen to have the other three, do you, or any other pieces of Barkie?

As the lady puts her handbag on the table and starts rummaging inside it the camera pans away to once again show Hugh standing at the front of the auction. By now Hugh has four monkeys about his person and his worry lines have thickened.

HUGH   Well, being in Coventry (repeat cheer as above) with its pubs, off licences, you'd expect to see some vintage wines or antiques associated with the brewing industry. So let's see what Susanne's come up with.

CUT TO   Yet another table. Sat at the table are the two humorous 'booze' characters (Vic and Bob – see Food and Drink *from Show 1) and 37-year-old power-dressed antique booze expert.*

EXPERT   So, fellas, what have you brought me today?

VIC & BOB   Sooze . . . booze. *(Vic and Bob then proceed to place a bottle of anonymous dusty brown home brew style booze on to the table.)*

EXPERT   Aah, looks interesting . . . Where did you get this?

DEREK   Our father left us it in his will . . . Just thought you might be able to tell us what type of booze it is, Sooze.

EXPERT   (examining bottle) Well there's no label . . .

WOMAN WITH BABY IN QUEUE   Aye, you two, can I have some of that booze for t' baby?

CHESTER   You can't give a baby booze!

DEREK   Yeah, you can't give baby booze, sorry Sooze, you were saying . . .

EXPERT   Ah, hold on, there is a label, yes, beneath the dust, er . . . it's Babycham.

DEREK & CHESTER   Babycham.

CHESTER   Hey, love, it's booze for a baby, come on (as they both motion to the lady with the baby to return to the table).

DEREK   Babycham . . . It's booze for a baby.

CUT TO   Hugh, who now has now got six monkeys attached to his person.

HUGH   You can't give a baby booze . . . Let's see what Whiskey and Brandy Bolland have got for us this week.

Whiskey and Brandy (Bob and Vic) are stood on a raised semicircular platform upon which are a Queen Anne chair, an antique dresser and an MFI pine-veneered double wardrobe. Vic and Bob are stood either side of the wardrobe. They are wearing matching suits with the trouser gussets approximately one foot too low. They both have an aluminium pan attached to a metal hook on the back of their jackets. They speak in gorgeous soft Scottish accents coincidentally very similar to the accent of the executive producer of this programme, Mr Mike Bolland.

BRANDY   Thank you, Hugh, yes, this week, we've found this magnificent wardrobe.

WHISKEY   It may not look that impressive but this wardrobe actually belongs to a very famous man indeed, doesn't it, Brandy?

BRANDY   Indeed it does, Whiskey, for this wardrobe belongs to American pop singer Prince.

WHISKEY   And how do we know this, Brandy?

Brandy and Whiskey firstly point out that the front of the wardrobe has only been painted to a height of 2 feet and the handles are fitted 6 inches from the floor. Whiskey opens the wardrobe doors to reveal a collection of small clothes from the Action Man and Ken range. For example, his frog diving suit with a high heel on the flipper, his school uniform which is 4 inches high, and his romper suit which is actually already on a slide in a microscope which is on a shelf in the wardrobe. (Pre-recorded shot of tiny romper suit as seen through microscope lens.)

At the base of the wardrobe is a termite mound. Brandy happens to know that Prince spends much of his spare time inside the mound curing hams. Vic knocks on the mound to see if Prince is home. The knock startles Prince and we hear his voice exclaim 'Hell's bells' and his leg shoots out of the side of the mound. Brandy immediately grabs the leg and pulls out Prince. Prince is in a black cape and gown and, when pulled out by Brandy clutching a nice cured ham, scuttles off stage singing, 'Alphabet Street'. (NB Prince of course is a child extra who is positioned behind the wardrobe lying down so that he can easily be pulled forward through the shell of the mound.)

CUT TO   Hugh now barely visible through a sea of 24 monkeys.

HUGH   'That's all from Coventry (cheers from audience as above). Join us next week when the Antiques Roadshow will be visiting the Cornetto Observation Centre, Gravesend. Goodnight, my friends.'

Closing titles show the monkeys gradually float off Hugh and commence floating, swooping and hovering around him like so many butterflies flitting around the erect member of a young doorman lying on a wooden pallet outside Zambeezies nightclub in Hartlepool. When a monkey gets too near to Hugh's head he snaps at it with his teeth as a pike might when snapping at a fig roll carelessly dropped into the lake by a bear that's too wrapped up in hopping and skipping to look after the contents of his handbag. Over the poignant image the following titles are run:

WRITTEN BY

Apricot of the Lighthearted Brigade
Professor Horsepeanut and the Numbskulls
Lieutenant Loobrush of Crumplybosoms
Noel Edmonds of Crinkley Bottom

PRODUCTION TEAM

Camera   The Singing Egg
Lights   The Whistling Beret
Sound   The Yodelling Hacksaw

Cutlery supplied by 'Dark Side of The Spoon'

Special housing for Mr Skully's model electronic helicopters supplied by 'How's Your Chopper'

A Bruin the Bear production for Channel Timothy

NB *The music for the above titles should be a beautiful baroque chamber piece.*

CUT TO

THE CHOKER

Vic and Bob in studio (positioned as before). Bob has now adopted the classic choker presentation stance. He now has an ink choker drawn on his neck.

VIC   It looks a lot better on you, Bob.

BOB   Do you think so? . . . And you say I can have it for £300.

VIC   Yeah.

BOB   I'll take it then. *(Bob hands over £300.)* What a beauty *(he is rubbing the choker and the ink is coming off on his hands)*. It fits so good . . . it feels like I'm not even wearing it.

VIC   Come on, Bob, we can't hang around here all night admiring your new choker.

Vic puts his arm around Bob and begins to guide him towards the desk. As they walk Bob continues to rabbit on about his choker whilst Vic (to camera) visually celebrates hoodwinking Bob into buy the ink drawing.

BOB   Vic, I'm just going to show me choker to the wife.

VIC   OK, Bob.

Bob exits stage. This celebration ends with Vic's clenched fists raised in the manner that a tennis player might on playing the winning shot of a long and nailbiting, arduous and tense, heroic and ultimately pointless rally.

Vic sits behind desk.

Enter Bob in Revenge Mode.

Bob presents his whelk-locating clothes horse. This is an old-fashioned wooden clothes horse with a daisy attached to it. It also has a car handbrake attached to it.

Bob asks Vic to cry out, 'Where is my whelk?'

At this Bob releases the handbrake and flies off to locate a whelk placed conveniently on the set.

Bob returns the whelk to Vic. Vic thanks him. Exit Bob.

Vic is staring at the whelk in the palm of his hand . . .

VIC   Wait a minute, Bob, this is not my whelk. This whelk is Dutch.

GREG MITCHELL

Vic now lays behind the desk and up pops Greg Mitchell, the lovely, cuddly sandy-coloured Labrador.

GREG   Hello, Greg Mitchell here. Talking about our friends the Dutch, I've just been down to that fancy Dutch holiday travel agents and booked me and the family on a coach trip to Holland for three weeks to see thousands and thousands *(realization of error leading to voice change)* and thousands of bloody tulips . . . Oh Gawd, what have I done? . . . my wife's going to kill me.

CORKY   *(the trilbied greyhound pops up)* Three weeks staring at tulips, Gregory. . . . I don't understand it.

GREG   Don't rub it in, Corky, I'm in enough truoble as it is . . . Get out. *(Greg swipes Corky with his paw as they both glide back behind the desk.)*

Up pops Vic again and entertains the viewer with 22 seconds of ripe Snackpot. On emerging from behind the desk he is eating from the packet of a savoury snack such as the Wotsit or the Cheesy. He is blowing the crushed snack from his mouth in the manner that Bruce Forsyth might do so.

VIC   What do you call that effect . . . It's not crumbing . . . Is it dusting, chalking? . . . A light flouring, even a corn storm . . . I don't know . . . Do you? . . . All I know is it feels like making love . . .

ELEPHANT MAN DREAM SEQUENCE

Opening shot is as per Shaftesbury Avenue dream sequence.

We look down to the lecturer who is finishing his lecture. Behind him is a white screen, behind which we can see the silhouette of what is apparently the elephant man. NB At this point we should cheat a little and make the silhouette look like it is actually the elephant man.

LECTURER   *(with voice muffled but still intelligible)* And now we reveal my final triumph.

The lecturer requests that the nurse pull back the screen.

She pulls back the screen.

We hear the audience gasp.

We see the lecturer with an expression on his face that says, 'There you are, what did I tell you?'

Camera reveals the collection of hardware behind the screen with a sign behind it saying, 'New wing of National Gallery'.

The audience applaud.

Camera turns on section of audience to reveal . . . wait for it . . . it's coming soon . . . hold your horses . . . hey, cool it . . . don't be impatient . . . all things come to yea who waits . . . bide your time . . . yes, it's . . . can you guess? . . . here it comes . . .

It's going to be great . . .

. . . have you guessed yet? . . . turn over . . . here it is . . .

Men with heads of sweetcorn.

CELEBRITY GUEST: BERT (BOOM-BANG-A-BANG) REYNOLD

BOB   And now, please welcome our very special guest, Bert Reynold (Burt Reynolds).

Enter Vic stage left. He is wearing a gingham tablecloth cape and holding it in front of him to partially obscure his face. He is drinking from a 2-litre Flora oil bottle. He is wearing large, red, industrial, lined rubber gloves.

He has a Gaffa tape moustache and on his head a special wig helmet that:

1 *Allows the skull to gently undulate as he speaks.*

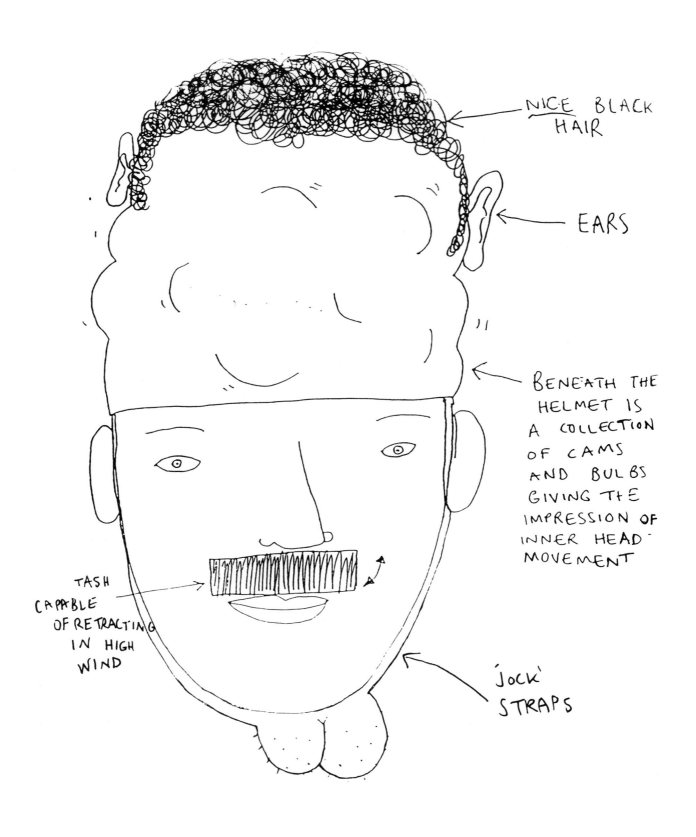

NICE BLACK HAIR

EARS

BENEATH THE HELMET IS A COLLECTION OF CAMS AND BULBS GIVING THE IMPRESSION OF INNER HEAD MOVEMENT

TASH CAPABLE OF RETRACTING IN HIGH WIND

'JOCK' STRAPS

BERT ("BOOM-BANG-A-BANG") REYNOLD

2 Allows a light to come on inside the skull if required (see drawing).

Vic settles on his seat. As he does so, he ejaculates 'hot diggidy dog, boy, what's this, a critter?' This is because he has apparently sat on a squirrel that was resting on his seat smoking a pipe (in fact, it wasn't actually quite lit . . . he was just 'thumbing' the rough-cut shag, probably Tamplet, into the bowl of the pipe).

Vic then withdraws his cape, revealing underneath a bib which is clearly stained with cooking oil.

Bob then interviews Vic. Questions may include the following:

BOB First off, Bert, can we hear your marvellous catchphrase?

BERT Yes . . . boom bang a bang.

BOB If you came home and found a shepherd in your living-room staring at the wall, would you:
a) ignore him
b) phone the police

BERT Neither, I would give him a strict ten min. deadline and if he hadn't stopped his staring and a gazing when the ten min. was up, I'd attract the attention of a neighbour, not in a flamboyant way with a flag or owt, but, in a nice gentle way with oh . . . a Jew's harp . . . or a beautiful lute . . . or a waft of aftershave and ask them what I should do . . .

BOB Bert, what's your favoured method of draught exclusion?

BERT Sausage dog.

BOB But that's a small puff pastry with meat in it.

BERT Damn right, boy, boom bang a bang, that's what I use.

BOB What about outdoors?

BERT I generally stand behind a cow.

BOB Bert, are you making a movie?

BERT Yes.

BOB Bert, if you're out in the woods and you find a plum in a beautiful sunkissed clearing, would you take it home or just leave it there to rot?

BERT Hold on, there's a lovely deer in this clearing, isn't there?

BOB Yes, it's just walked in now.

BERT And is there a little baby deer?

BOB Yes, but it's stillborn.

BERT Shit, man . . . Hey, maybe it was killed by eating one of the other plums.

BOB Could be.

BERT It's not safe to leave it then.

BOB Yeah, but if you take it home, you might poison one of your own kids.

BERT It's a dilemma all right. Maybe I'd just attract someone's attention and ask them what to do.

BOB But you'd have to be careful not to frighten the deer.

BERT You're goddamn right, boy, and I haven't got me Jew's harp with me . . . I could stand there waving a twig over the plum till someone passed by . . . but I could be here for months . . . where is this forest?

BOB *(consulting paper)* Middle of nowhere.

BERT How big is it then?

BOB About the size of Portugal or one of those stripped countries, e.g. Chile.

BERT I might starve . . . How long does it take for a plum to rot?

47

BOB About five months.

BERT Well, I'll kill the deer then and eat that.

BOB Thank you, Bert.

BERT Thank you, boy.

Bob and Vic get up and leave stage and dance into

SONG: 'LET'S TAKE A LOOK AT IT'

VIC I love the smell of onion bhajees

BOB I love the smell of the Nigel Benn's car keys

VIC I love the smell of Pol Pot's dungarees

VIC & BOB So come on now, let's have a look at it
Come on now let's have a sniff of it
Come on now let's look a little bit more

DA DA DOM DI DOM DI
DOM DE DOM DA DA

DOM DI DOM DI DOM DE DOM
DA DA

BOB I love the smell of Kung Fu

VIC I love the smell of Whipsnade zoo

BOB I love the smell of Lulu's hairdo

VIC & BOB So come on now, let's have a look at it
Come on now let's have a sniff of it
Come on now let's look a little bit more

DA DA DOM DI DOM DI
DOM DE DOM DA DA

DOM DI DOM DI DOM DE DOM
DA DA

VIC I love the smell of shredded corduroy

BOB I love the smell of hoi palloi

VIC I love the smell of boiled boy

VIC & BOB So come on now, let's have a look at 'em
Come on now let's have a sniff of 'em
Come on now let's look a little bit more
Come on now let's have a look at 'em
So come on now let's have a sniff of 'em
Come on now let's look a little bit more

THE BRA MEN: 'THE MILKMAN COLLECTS HIS MONEY'

Exterior of modern semi-detached in the Brookside mould. A milkman is at the door and rings the bell.

Door is answered by Dave who bends down to pick up his milk delivery. He looks up to see the milkman still standing there with his payment book and pen.

DAVE All right, mate?

MILKMAN Hello. Can we settle up?

DAVE Aye, sure, mate.

Dave then looks up to the milkman and gives him a look that suggests 'are you trying to look at my breasts?' His hand clutches the top of his shirt to close any gap that might be seen down.

DAVE *(getting up)* You trying to look at me bra, mate?

MILKMAN *(laughingly)* No.

DAVE Oh, you think it's funny, do you? . . . Big joke, is it, wearing a bra? . . .. You make me sick, your type . . . You can keep your milk.

Dave shuts door, taking with him the two pints of milk that were on the step. The milkman walks back up the drive bemused, confused and slightly unfulfilled. As he leaves, he passes Pat on the driveway. Pat confronts him in this manner.

PAT You laughing at me, mate? . . . Something funny, is there?

SHOW

NB This show is a have a cup of tea special in which at every available opportunity participants will be holding a cup and saucer in their hands.

OPENING TITLES

Yes, another show commences. This time we remember the pain that certain people had to endure during the last week of August 1956 . . . Having said that, the first two weeks of January 1963 were no bed of roses . . .

1 Trick photography used to confuse Dutch cyclist.

2 Ditch dug near figgy smell.

3 Boy genius draws up plans for new type of peanut.

4 Callanetics teacher has nightmare near franking machine.

5 Pease pudding marketing board calls it a day.

6 Short man envies tall man's short wife.

7 Midget gems clog up experimental computer.

8 Clown blamed for erotic woodcarving.

9 Angel seen flying near Kiwi shoe polish factory.

10 Helicopter pilot swoops down for closer look at lucky rabbit's foot.

11 Local publican suspects one of his bar staff has beriberi, but the question is which one . . .?

VOICE-OVER Ladies and gentlemen, see if you can guess as we welcome . . . Reeves and Mortimer!

Vic and Bob emerge and sing the following song. Behind them is the hunchback from Show 1 *carrying a banner, this time declaring the word* 'NIGHTIE'. *He walks across the stage and back again.*

SONG

1 Hello,
we're a couple of girls
Hello,
lipstick and curls.

We read *Woman's Own*,
tidy up round the home
and brass was used for coins in Roman Britain.

2 I'm Julie,
I'm the one with the limp.
I'm Carol,
I too have a limp.

We read Marie Claire,
And shop at Fine Fare,
And the Dutch have no concept of rust.

3 I'm married to a man with one lung.
I'm shacked up with a man with one plum.

We watch Neighbours at one
And then at half five.
And the Cornish tin mine industry's defunct.

POP NEWS

Vic and Bob then take up their positions behind the desk and introduce themselves and the show.

VIC Have you got any deodorant?

BOB Yes.

VIC Well put some on, will you.

BOB That's very funny, that.

VIC Took car for a service yesterday.

BOB Did it pass?

VIC No, I couldn't get it through the church doors.

BOB I've got a load of letters here from Jimmy Nail. What should I do with them?

VIC Just mark them return to Spender.

BOB Vic, please give me some up-to-date pop news.

VIC All right, Bob, I will . . . If you like your rock hot, Annie Lennox has decided to move to Texas . . .

BOB Which branch?

VIC Newton Abbot.

BOB Bryan Ferry has moved to Iceland.

VIC Which branch?

BOB Newton Abbot.

VIC Midge Ure has moved into my mum's.

BOB Which branch?

VIC What do you think?

BOB Newton Abbot.

VIC Correct. Next?

Vic and Bob both put on checked tweedy fishing hats and hold two fishing rods.

BOB *(holding up an LP record cover by the white reggae group Long House Mat)* Vic, next a record review. Have you had a chance to listen to the new album by Long House Mat?

VIC Yes, it's piffle.

BOB What, you're poo pahing it?

VIC It's got no parf parf.

BOB So you're poo pahing it for lack of parf parf.

VIC Yes, it lacks oomph parf parf.

BOB But it's got pazzaz.

VIC It may have pazzaz but I'm poo pahing it for lack of oomph and panache.

BOB Hold on, Vic, you're causing a brouhaha due to lack of ooomph and poo pahing Long House Mat's snazzy new offering.

VIC I'll poo pah you, you nincompoop, if I want to cause a broo ha ha over lack of oomph parf parf I will do, you ninny.

BOB Thanks, Vic . . . Later on we've got a boy genius who will be revealing his plans for a new type of peanut that's very long . . . almost too long . . . See what you think anyway.

VIC And we've got Alice Cooper and the Starship Trooper with his Pooper Scooper. *(As Vic delivers this line he is interrupted by Uncle Peter.)*

FIGHTING MEN

PETER Ooh no, ooh my.

VIC What is it, Peter?

PETER I'm going to blurt.

VIC Well go on then, blurt it out.

PETER Blurt.

BOB Peter, calm down. Just blurt out what you've got to blurt.

PETER *(pointing to the two fighting men who are again fighting each other, as per* Show 1*)* Blurt, blurt.

BOB Brilliant. Scrap on.
Vic and Bob proceed towards the fighters encouraging the audience to chant 'Fight, fight' as they do so.

VIC Hold on. Break it up, break it up. What are you fighting about now?

1ST FIGHTER My good friend ordinary seaman Mick Box claims that plums bring good luck.

2ND FIGHTER Whereas my colleague able seaman Lee Kerslake insists that it is the apricot that brings good luck.

BOB I'm sorry, lads, I haven't a clue . . . I wish I did know.

VIC Let's see if our resident experts Marvin Gaye and Otis Redding can shed any light on this . . . Otis, Marvin, plum or apricot – which one's the luckier?

CUT TO

OTIS AND MARTIN

OTIS Hold your horses, Vic . . . We're on the dock of the bay again watching a big red tanker coming in from Germany . . . We're not quite sure what it's bringing in . . . Probably those German Shepherd dogs . . .

MARVIN Yes, we reckon there's about 2000 of the dogs on board. They will probably be fed on sauerkraut by fräuleins wearing gingham and drinking beer.

OTIS Yes, Marvin, the dogs will probably be forced on deck by Luger-wielding SS officers shouting 'schnell schnell swinehund essen der sauerkraut'.

MARVIN Anyway, Vic, the truth of the matter is that both these lads are suffering unnecessary sexual guilt triggered off by their anxiety over their bulemia.

OTIS That's very clear. They're using lucky fruits as a substitute for their impotence.

MARVIN Our leaflet on baldness may help.

At this point an aston flashes in the bottom corner of screen saying '£4.99'.

OTIS In the meantime, it being a sexual problem, why not listen to the wise words of the sexual conquistador himself . . . our good friend Mr Barry White.

Otis and Marvin turn to either the right or left-hand side depending on certain as yet unexplained sounds emanating from certain heaps of dung deposited in certain people's attics . . . YOU KNOW WHO YOU ARE. Anyway this head movement will be either swift or slow depending on certain as yet unexplained vibrations emanating from certain deadbeats, beatniks and bums gathering round a certain as yet unembroidered curtain in Dudley . . . YOU KNOW WHO YOU ARE . . . and ye shall inherit the world for it is written thrice over tenfold in . . . (at this point Rick Parfitt of Status Quo strode into our office, grabbed the typewriter with his denim-covered fingers and hurled it furiously into the dung-filled street below, where peasants mingled noisily selling their roughly hewn clay hats to one another).

CUT TO

BARRY WHITE'S NEW VIDEO

Firstly, let us say that if anyone really wants to know what the following video looks like all they need do is obtain a copy of the Rod Stewart video for 'Tonight's the night' starring Rod Stewart and Brigg Elkland. But if your telly has been repossessed or your glasses are inexplicably covered in bird lime then the following instructions should be adhered to:

Two Georgian chesterfield-style wing chairs are positioned face to face in front of an impressive black gothic fireplace. A real fire is raging in the

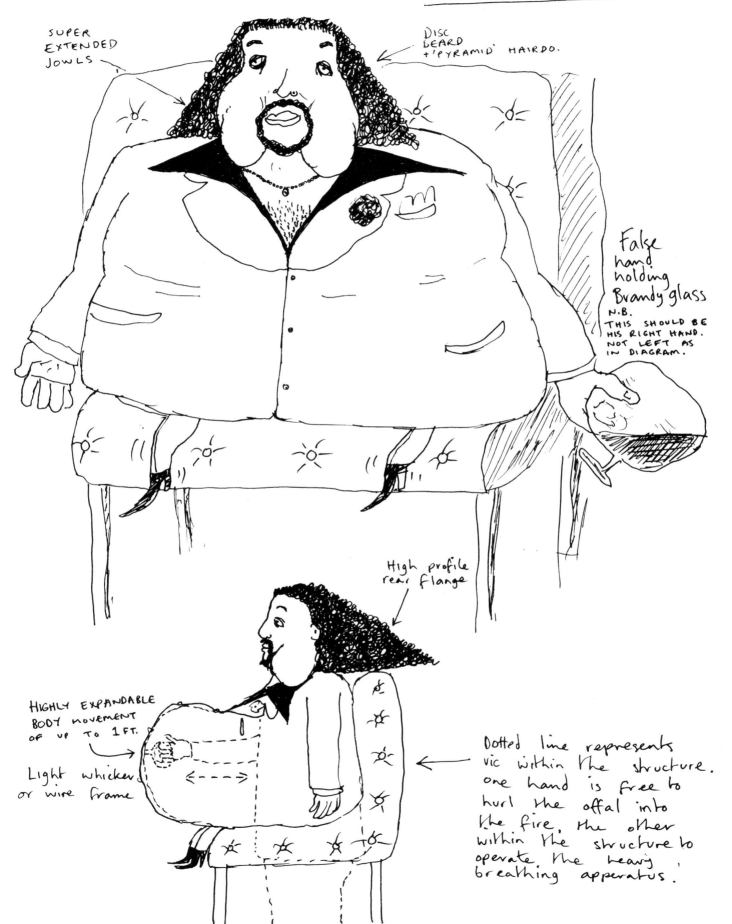

BARRY 'WHITE'

SUPER EXTENDED JOWLS

DISC BEARD +'PYRAMID' HAIRDO.

False hand holding Brandy glass
N.B. THIS SHOULD BE HIS RIGHT HAND. NOT LEFT AS IN DIAGRAM.

High profile rear flange

HIGHLY EXPANDABLE BODY MOVEMENT OF UP TO 1 FT.

Light whicker or wire frame

Dotted line represents vic within the structure. one hand is free to hurl the offal into the fire. the other within the structure to operate the heavy breathing apperatus.

hearth, its flames licking the walls of the chimney giving the impression of a room filled with flitting and darting satsumas, frivolous daredevil tangerines and flirty dancing mandarins.

On one seat is Barry White (Vic) (see drawing). On the other seat is a lady with long blonde hair and a red evening dress. NB this lady's face is not seen until the end of the video.

Barry is holding a large glass of brandy (the brandy glass itself is very large as opposed to it being a 'large' brandy). By the side of Barry, on an occasional table, is a plate of offal. During the course of the song Barry alternately slaps a piece of offal on to the fire and sprays a stream of lighter fuel into the flames. Vic also, with his free hand (see drawing) operates his stomach to give the impression of heavy stomach breathing.

Vic has written a piece of original music which may need to be professionally recorded.

'Ohh, That's Great!'

Oh, love, you're looking great sitting there like
   that,
and I bet you fancy me an' all.
Loosen your blouse, love, so I can see the top of
   your bra.
Oh, that's great that, love,
I'm going to kiss you any minute now so get your
   lips pursed up all ready.
Oh, that's great.
Just looking at you I can tell you go like the
   clappers,
Now show us your knockers,
Oh, they're great.
Come on, get your knickers off.

(At this point the lady turns around to camera revealing that she is in fact . . . a pineapple).

NB During the above video there are Chart Show style graphic facts on screen giving the following information about the White character:

1 Barry thinks the turtle of Turtle Wax is 'real cute' and writes to him every day. Barry hopes that one day 'Turt' as he calls him will star in his own TV cartoon series.
2 Barry is DEAD posh.
3 Barry only has about five pints on a night out in his local, BUT HE DOESN'T HALF GO THROUGH THE CRISPS.
4 Clever Barry wrote the Highway Code on the back of a duck in a beehive.
5 Barry's famous disc beard is achieved by shaving around a tin of butterbeans.

CUT TO

THE HORSE

Back in the studio Vic is standing with Uncle Peter and the two fighting men. Bob is trapped under a horse which is sat on him.

VIC So there you are, fellas . . . Was any of that helpful?

1ST FIGHTER Yes, deep down we both knew that it was a sexual problem.

2ND FIGHTER Yes, and by way of a thank-you please accept this tiny revolving tool kit.

Fighter holds out the palm of his hand towards Vic. There appears to be nothing on it. Camera goes into extreme close-up of the palm of the hand and sure enough we see on it a tiny revolving tool kit.

Vic takes the revolving tool kit and half heartedly thanks the men. The men begin to leave the stage one in front of the other shuffling as if in a large queue outside a hotel where it is rumoured that the proprietor is giving away free metal objects.

VIC (with slightly interested look to camera) Revolving tools.

UNCLE PETER (*pointing to Bob*) Donkey.

VIC (*surprised*) Eh?

BOB (*emotionlessly*) Help.

UNCLE PETER Donkey.

VIC Eh?

BOB Help.

As you will notice the above dialogue has a natural rhythm to it which is exploited firstly by the three comedians and then enhanced by an experienced professional drummer (with kit).

The sort of experience the drummer will require might be, for example:

1 Three weeks in a garage band 'learning the ropes'.
2 Victory in drum competition organized by the manufacturers of 'the Wheetie'.
3 One month drumming for the amazing Constipated Sue during her summer season at Pontins, Morecambe Bay.
4 Six-month whistle-stop tour of the States with rock giants Gulls Balls.
5 Twenty-five years with The Who.

Vic prances across the stage to find out what is wrong with Bob. The answer seems simple: he is trapped under a horse. But is this how the comedians see it?

VIC (*to horse*) Help . . . Yes, but what's the hurry, loosen up . . . You horses are all the same . . . always want to be first past the post . . . What's your problem here?

BOB Help, help, help, help (*ad nauseam until halted by Vic*).

Vic gradually realizes it is not the horse requiring assistance and crawls round it to where Bob's head is and stares quizzically at Bob's head as he continues to cry 'Help'.

BOB Well.

VIC Well what?

BOB Have you tasted your tea?

VIC (*tasting his tea*) Oh, it's got sugar in it.

BOB Yes, it's mine now, give it here.

Vic and Bob continue to sip their tea as they stare vacantly away, occasionally smiling at each other. After slightly too long:

BOB Vic.

VIC What?

BOB It's him again (*pointing to the stage floor where the man under the ice is still furiously seeking assistance, this time, of course, whilst enjoying a nice cup of tea and a digestive*).

VIC Hello, what's the matter? Do you want a top up? (*Indicating motion of tea pot.*)

BOB Another biscuit?

VIC & BOB Oh, he's off.

At this cry the two comedians crawl quickly in unison across the floor of the stage in an attempt to follow the path of the man under the ice. Simultaneous to their departure the horse rears up and scarpers, shouting:

HORSE Nay nay (*pre-recorded comedy voice-over*).

After scarpering around for an appropriate time, (e.g. the time it takes to take the top off a biro and place it in a drawer about 8 ft away, or the time it takes to draw a rough outline of a pram on a (previously numbed) swallow's neck, or the average time that a Greek ferryman can bear receiving a chinese burn from a TV repair girl) the two comedians rise up sharply declaring:

VIC & BOB We've lost him.

Mulligan and O'Hare

Moods

A collection of "mood" melodies all of which point out the terror and confusion that occurs during periods of obscured vision

The Day The Donkey Derby came to Town
People came to watch from all around
But us, we didn't see who won the race
As the supergroup The Who swooped down from the
moon and squirted tart lemon in our eye/face!

But for the Plate Fungus (Rock operetta)

I'm over here
I'm over here
And I'm up here so high in the tree
Oh my friend can you see me?
No my friend I can't see you
as this plate fungus obscures my view

MY ROSE HAS LEFT ME
IM IN A MOOD
shes gone to Kenya
~~with~~ with the Bloke
From ALLIED CARPETS
she wasn't inmunised
Thats a LEGAL
      requirement
She's increasingly slapdash
          (become)
Since we bought that
NEW HEARTH RUG.

Frustrated by Weeds

As I gaze into a pool to receive
a reflection of me
I'm ultimately Frustrated by the presence of too many
                                              weeds.
How ever much I try
to push them aside
They Constantly
return to
Frustrate ME!

ANOTHER DAY IN PARADISE

LE NEZ DE LA
HUNKY HOMME
FRANCAISE.
I am me, and you are
            you.
And you are I, and I
            am too.
But somebody obscures
my view of you.
Really who?.
GERALD DEPARDEIUE.

LINK TO

THE BRA MEN: 'AT THE TRAVEL AGENTS'

We are at the counter of the travel agents. A sign behind the counter indicates that the travel agent is called Bottsman Travel. Pat and Dave are being attended to by a young lady.

LADY   There you are, sirs, your travel tickets for two weeks on the isle of Grief.

DAVE   Oh, thanks, love, that's great.

PAT   I was just wondering, love, are there any . . . you know . . . er, topless beaches on Grief?

LADY   Oh yes, there are lots of topless beaches for the ladies.

DAVE   What do you mean . . . there's none for the fellas like us then?

LADY   Well, it wouldn't make any difference for you two.

PAT   Oh aye, you're saying we're flat like.

DAVE   'Ere, are you saying we've got nowt worth showing?

LADY   *(laughing)* Honestly.

PAT   Oh, you think it's funny, do you . . . you got a problem with us wearing bras?

DAVE   It's a big joke to you, innit? . . . come on, Pat, we're leaving . . . you can keep your bloody tickets.

Pat and Dave leave with tickets.

CUT TO

LADY   What did you make of that, Ray?

The lady turns to look at her colleague, but sees that he is laid on the floor with a knife in his chest. He is just freshly dead. On seeing this, the lady immediately starts screaming (still sat in seat) with her hands and head shaking in the style of loosely operated marionette.

To accompany this scene is a sting of frightening orchestral music.

REEVES AND MORTIMER PRODUCTS

CUT TO   Vic and Bob join Uncle Peter centre stage with the visual display board introducing some of the latest Reeves and Mortimer products.

Cowboy Soil Vibrating Unit

This cowboy has a special prong that when inserted into any item will gently vibrate it.

Use it to vibrate your house and thereby knock all the accumulated dust (or, in winter, snow) off your roof.

If you receive an unexpected family visit insert it into the family pet to keep the children amused.

Also features suction probe that will suck up previously vibrated water and filter it via the cowboy's liver. It is then stored within the cowboy's leg where it is available on tap for a thirsty boy or pet.

Buy two and vibrate the whole village.

Can also wake you up in the morning by vibrating your cutlery drawer.

Bob asks Vic why he would want to vibrate his house let alone the whole village.

Vic has no answer and accuses Bob of always looking at the detail and not taking a wider view. Vic rips the display drawing off the board in disgust.

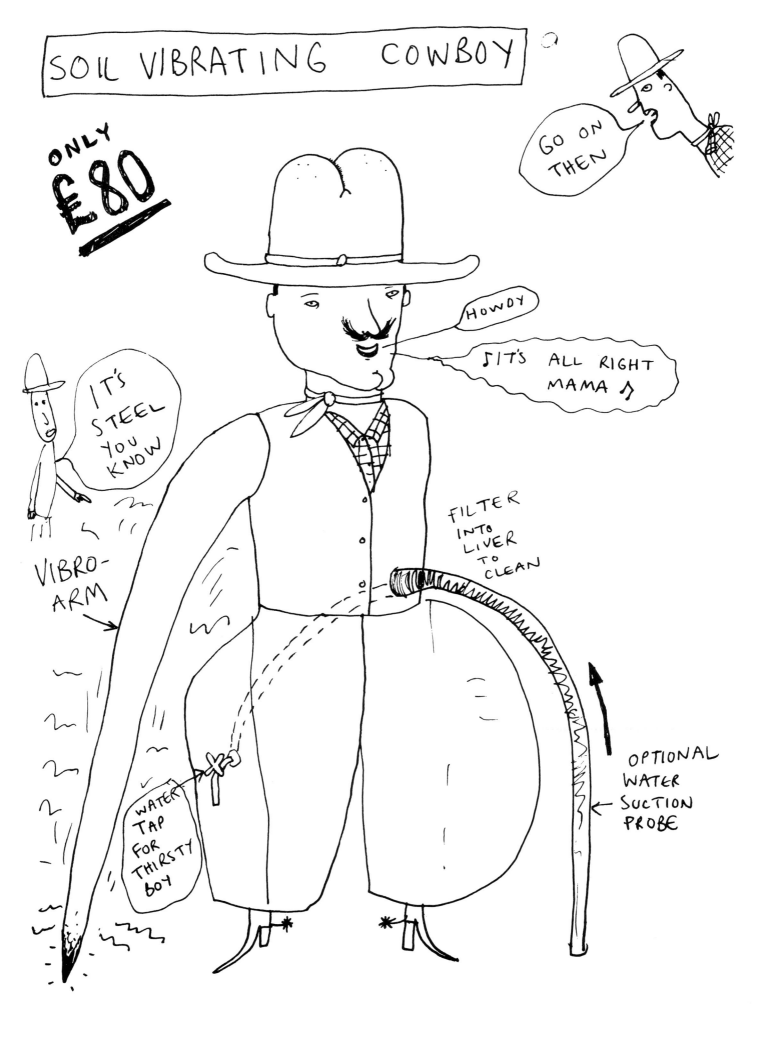

New 'Walk Me Home' Cheddar

Bob is shown out on a date with Sharon out of Eastenders. Vic doesn't know who Sharon is. Bob tries to explain. Vic eventually clocks who she is when Bob illustrates the peculiar whistle that Sharon has.

After a night at the theatre your date is killed by a sniper's bullet or by a shadowy figure wielding a broken bottle.

BOB   Oh I don't like the sound of that . . . Imagine if he cut you and it took ages to die and you were on the way to the bookies . . . Yeah, I'd rather be sniped . . . Yeah, a shadowy figure . . . But who is it? . . . Could be the lighting man . . . The stage hand . . . An irate electrician . . . Or even a spurned plumber . . . Jesus, it could be you! . . . I don't like the sound of it . . . Let's stick with the sniper.

VIC   Anyway you're stuck with no one to walk you home . . . Unless that is you've invested in a new R & M 'Walk Me Home' Cheddar . . . And there he is . . . With his simple cry, 'Don't worry no more, missy. I'm Uncle Ched and I'll walk you home. Oh yes, maam' . . .

BOB   But, Vic, how does this Cheddar walk?

VIC   No idea, Bob . . . *(faces camera)* but it does.

BOB   These are some of the products that are currently under development at the Reeves and Mortimer secret factory at Unit 4, Chappeldale Industrial Estate, Whitstable, Kent.

VIC   *(angrily)* Bob, get over here. Look, the factory is now no longer secret. You might as well tell them that the registration number of that car we used in the Reading robbery was NHN 908E.

BOB   Ah Vic, you're just as bad as me, man, you've given it away.

VIC   Don't be daft, that wasn't the real number.

BOB   Of course, it was NHN 908P.

VIC   *(with raised hand)* Why, I ought to . . . If I have to give that kid his gloves back you're paying.

The Will Duplicating Sink

VIC   This sink will duplicate any will just like a photocopier only better.

BOB   How does it work?

VIC   I don't know. It just does.

Pen Retrieval Cork

VIC   If your pen drops into a tin of paint or into a well full of blood, simply write the letter 'L' on the side of the cork and throw it at the moon. Your pen will miracously leap out of the paint, or blood, and back into your suit pocket.

BOB   Any proof?

VIC   None whatsoever.

NB *The above two products are simply described verbally without the use of drawings on the visual display unit.*

BEIGE CARPET

Enter Uncle Peter carrying a 20 ft roll of beige carpeting (i.e. carpet stuck to cardboard roll so that it is light enough to be easily carried).

VIC   Yes. My lucky beige carpet. 30ft of beige good luck.

Yes, but no need to rely on good luck once you've converted your lucky carpet into the hydrovelt.

Yes, simply stick a picture of a thirsty cowboy on to your lucky beige slab and it instantly converts

into the hydrovelt and will pump literally thousands of gallons of salt water on to anyone daft enough to get in your way (this is illustrated by a drawing of the hydrovelt being used to knock a shepherd off the roof of a house).

BOB   Why would anyone want to do that?

VIC   I've no idea . . . (to camera) but they do.

At end of display, Bob pushes the unit off stage revealing Uncle Peter standing with his trousers round his ankles staring at a pineapple.

VIC   Peter!

PETER   What is it?

VIC   A pineapple.

PETER   Thank God you stopped me in time. You won't send me back for this, will you?

VIC   No, Peter, now just go back to bed.

PETER   Will you tuck me in, please?

VIC   OK.

Uncle Peter leaves stage.

Vic and Bob sing the following song. Original music provided to be pre-recorded by a band with an experienced guitarist. Appropriate experience in this context would be:

1 First band Mixed Grill.
2 Second band M1 Pile Up (with drummer from Mixed Grill).
3 Third band Lock Stock and Carol, specializing in Carol King covers and incorporating the brass section from Stop Making Scent.
4 Fourth band Mixed Grill (with bassist from Pine Cone).

SONG: 'MY LUCKY CARPET'

VIC   It's my lucky carpet.

BOB   Yes.

VIC   Let met tell you how it started.

BOB   Go on, then.

VIC   I bought it in a market.

BOB   Who from?

VIC   A bloke who sells carpets.

BOB   Go on.

VIC   It's my underfelted lucky charm,
it's a lot more lucky than my lucky barn,
and if we were ever parted . . .

BOB   Yes?

VIC   I would be broken hearted,
lucky lucky carpet.

At this point Vic encourages the audience to clap along and sing the words 'lucky lucky carpet'.

VIC & BOB   Lucky lucky carpet.

Just prior to the end of the song Uncle Peter moves the product display board revealing sitting behind it on a stool a girl with long blonde hair (as in the Timotei ads) washing her hair in a bucket. Bob and Vic leap up into the air to mark the triumphant end of the song and at exactly the same time the Timotei girl whips her hair out of the bucket and into the air.

The camera freezes this shot. Vic, Bob and girl all have stupid expressions and the camera very quickly shows each of these expressions in turn.

BRITISH INFORMATION BOARD

This is a pre-recorded insert featuring the hilarious antics of Jack Dent and Eric Potter (see 'The Country Code' last show).

The titles should be as last week, but substitute a picture of sombre-looking factory for picture of haystack and the words 'health and safety at work' for 'the country code'.

The action takes place in an old heavy engineering works. This should be a busy place with the following minimum level of activities.

Machine shop
On and off loading facilities
Overhead cranes
Compressed air facilities
Well-stocked stores
Large containers full of parts
At least two levels
Loading bay
Canteen
Fork-lifts
Discarded parts and cancelled orders outdoor rotting area
Paint shop
Rhum carnet assembly facilities
Shot blaster

The above are of course not all essential but we hope that they help to give an idea of the sort of location required.

Scene One

NB The moment this insert starts an electronic clock commences timing the piece in the corner of the screen. It is an athletics type display which goes down to 100ths of seconds.

Bob is attempting to pierce Vic's ear using an industrial machine drill . . . you know the type where the operator stands and pulls the drill down using his right hand in the manner that one might operate an old-fashioned slot machine or pull a pint of real ale if one was a member of the dwarf family.

So anyway, we have a close-up of Bob operating machine . . . camera pulls back to show Vic's head ready to receive the drill.

VOICE-OVER   Hey, you.

VIC & BOB   What us?

VOICE-OVER   Are you attempting to pierce that young gentleman's ears?

BOB   Yes.

VOICE-OVER   Are you not aware that ear piercing without safety glasses can lead to loss of Kendal Mint Cake from top pocket?

Bob's hand immediately dashes to check the contents of his top pocket . . . You should just see his face when he realizes his mint cake is gone . . . TALK ABOUT DISAPPOINTMENT . . . Oh well.

Scene Two

Vic and Bob are hunting gazelle in the factory.

Opening shot is of an area of the factory with much machinery located around aisles. At first no action is seen. It is as if the camera is lying in wait for something to happen as in a wildlife documentary.

Suddenly Vic and Bob pop up alternately and extremely quickly in the manner of tribesmen popping up and peeking over bushes. Let's say each comedian pops up twice. They are both wielding African spears and shields (the latter made from animal hide).

VOICE-OVER   Hey, you.

No response from the comics. They still think they might not have been seen. Camera maintains vigil on machinery for four seconds only.

VOICE-OVER   Hey, you.

Camera maintains vigil for a further four seconds at which point our comics' eyes slowly appear over the machinery.

VOICE-OVER   Yes, you.
Our comics emerge in the way one would after having been, as it were, 'caught in the act'.

VOICE-OVER   Are you two stalking antelope?

VIC   Yes.

BOB   No.

VIC & BOB   (resignedly) Yes.

VOICE-OVER   Are you aware that the factory gazelle is a protected species and the stalking thereof can lead to loss or death of handbag crab?

Vic slowly raises handbag to chest height and nervously looks inside it, hardly bearing to find out the fate of his handbag crab. Look of intolerable grief and pain. He pulls out crab and shows it to Bob. They both take off their hats as a mark of respect. A couple of old male workers slowly approach them and offer their condolences.

Scene Three

Vic and Bob are practising the art of long distance cream cake administration. We see Vic in the factory yard at one end of an enormous stick (60 feet). Beside him is a group of five factory workers watching what he's doing. The other end of the stick is attached to Bob who is protruding from a fork lift truck's forks at their maximum height. He is lying on a fringed altar cloth and next to him is a ceremonial church style candle (see drawing).

NB *Hess is optional.*

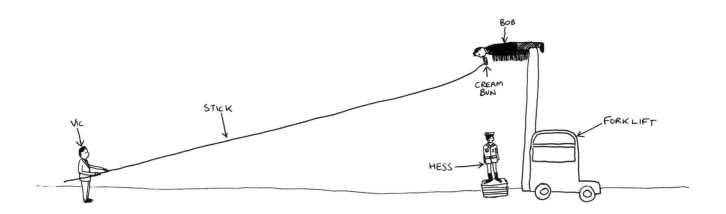

First shot is wide establishing shot. Second shot is of Vic from waist up making facial expressions that exemplify the British man toiling at his endeavours. Behind him we see the workers looking either vaguely interested or alternatively encouraging Vic gently as if they had placed a bet on the outcome of Vic's activities. Next shot zooms in to Bob's face where we see that a lovely chocolate éclair is being furiously rubbed against his face.

VOICE-OVER   Hey, you.

VIC   What, me?

VOICE-OVER   Yes, you. Is that your long distance ceremonial éclair administrating unit?

VIC   Yes.

VOICE-OVER   Don't you know that the ceremonial feeding of fresh cream fancies over distances greater than a furlong can lead to loss of respect from boxing promoters.

Suddenly a boxing promoter appears from nowhere. He looks like a slightly overweight bricklayer. He has a slightly feminine sideparting, very tight button-down shirt collar, thin tie with diagonal grey and pink stripes, tight grey double-breasted suit with slightly too long trousers and a nice pair of Nigerian oar shoes on his feet.

PROMOTER   (a white man trying to talk like a black man) Oi, Potter, listen up. You are out of your depth. I'll see to it you never box in this country no more. You are now very definitely personel non gratis, Potter. I treated you like my own son but I get nothing back from you, no respect or nothing . . . If you poke your weaselly face in my gym again I'll cut you.

At an appropriate point in above speech camera welts to Vic who is looking appropriately shamefaced and sheepish. (Promoter is seen during above speech over Potter's shoulder and

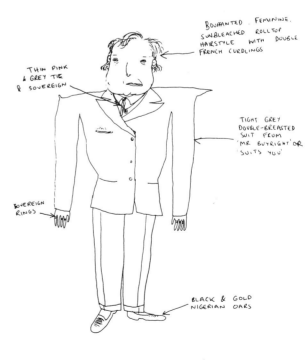

BOUFFANTED, FEMININE, SUNBLEACHED ROLLTOP HAIRSTYLE WITH DOUBLE FRENCH CURDLINGS

THIN PINK & GREY TIE & SOVEREIGN

TIGHT GREY DOUBLE-BREASTED SUIT FROM 'MR BUYRIGHT' OR 'SUITS YOU'

SOVEREIGN RINGS

BLACK & GOLD NIGERIAN OARS

ALAN PERRY
BOXING PROMOTIONS

out of focus; he is brought into sharp focus on delivery of last line, i.e. they are both looking at camera.)

Scene Four

Camera creeps up on our comics who are relaxing against a wall in some vaguely private area, e.g. behind skip, behind shed, down an alley, etc. Vic is holding a slice of Mr Kipling chocolate fudge cake on a paper plate. Bob is pouring Carnation milk on to the cake. As soon as the camera has got within earshot we hear this obscenity:

BOB   Say when.

VOICE-OVER   Hey, you.

VIC & BOB   *(turning to camera and irritated)* What?

VOICE-OVER   Are you wearing eyeshadow?

VIC & BOB   Yes. What of it?

VOICE-OVER   No . . . it's very nice . . . what shade is it?

VIC   It's Bluey Hue.

BOB   Isn't it Blue Huey?

VIC   Or is it Blue Poo? . . . Hold on, what's it got to do with you?

BOB   Yeah, will you leave us alone.

CUT TO   Silhouette of man in lobster costume standing on top of something near by that is quite high (i.e. 30 ft which is considered quite high these days). He is backlit in the manner that Spielberg might backlight if he was lighting up anything.

LOBSTER   In the fullness of time. But right now I'm going to rock. *(Two rock fireworks go off next to lobster accompanied by haunting heavy metal wail as the rock chords ring out around the factory.)*

CUT TO   End credits as per last show, but with the following actual credits.

A British Information Board Presentation
In association with Max Factor Cosmetics
Presented by Jack Dent and Eric Potter

Mr Dent and Mr Potter are currently appearing with Punt & Dennis in 'Baked Beany Baked Beany' at Mr Potty's lunchtime Sardine Club.

CUT TO

BOB'S FALL

BOB   *(falling pathetically)* Oh, Vic, I've fallen.

VIC   Bad luck, sir!

BOB   Bad luck indeed for not only have I fallen, but in doing so I have broken this leg . . . and this leg.

VIC   Both legs! That's double bad luck, sir. Have you considered carrying a lucky charm?

BOB   Yes, but they don't work.

VIC   Don't they?

CUT TO

SLADE IN RESIDENCE

JIM   All right, Noddy?

NODDY   All right?

NODDY (cont)   You should have seen that queue at the butchers. It took me three hours to get this meat.

JIM   That's crazy, Nod . . . I can imagine waiting three hours to get a ticket for US monster truck racing or something like that, but not meat . . .

NODDY I know . . . I go there early as well to get the best cuts.

JIM (looking at watch) Hold on, Nod, it's only nine o'clock now. What time did you get there?

NODDY Five o'clock.

JIM Five o'clock in the bloody morning, it doesn't open till eight.

NODDY I know, but there was a sale on, wasn't there? I tell you what though . . . whilst I was waiting, I saw one of those bubble cars . . . do you remember them?

JIM What . . . a bubble car . . . a car made out of a bubble . . .?

NODDY No . . . it's a proper car, but it looks a bit like a bubble . . . they look really great, they're only tiny . . . I tell you what, as well, the bloke driving it was either that bloke out of *French Connection Two* . . . Gene Backman, or if it wasn't him, it was the astrologer bloke with the curly perm off the tele . . . oh, what's his name?

JIM Duncan Grant.

NODDY Yeah, that's him.

Dave seen at the kitchen door with rubber gloves on and a handled pan scrubbing brush.

DAVE Hey up, Noddy . . . look, I'm trying this new washing-up liquid you got me at the sales, and to be honest I'm not impressed . . . it won't shift this Cup-A-Soup we had for dinner yesterday.

NODDY Oh, I'm sorry to hear that, Dave . . . but, look, stick at it . . . at least you know now.

DAVE Yes, I do know . . . to my cost . . . I've been trying to shift this Cup-A-Soup for three hours now.

JIM That's not a Cup-A-Soup, Dave . . . that's

red paint (holding up monster US truck). I was painting me US monster truck model last night.

JIM AND NODDY Aaaarrr . . . monster truck paint.

DAVE (exiting) You make me sick sometimes, you lot.

Enter Don Powell (holding rolled-up ball of newspaper).

DON Hey look, I've just bought a couple of puppies.

NODDY Don, that's a packet of chips.

DON I know, but I had you going, didn't I?

JIM AND NODDY No.

DON (looking at shopping bag) Oh great, did you get me my sausages?

NODDY Yes, two pork sausages for Don.

DON (panicking) But I wanted beef.

NODDY I know and I got you beef . . . but I had you going, didn't I?

Slade finger point administered on Don by Noddy and Jim.

NODDY (to Jim who is now concentrating on examining his fireworks) Oh, Jim, you got the fireworks in. Any good ones in there?

JIMMY Yeah, Nod, bostin'. Look . . . air bomb, genie of the lamp, Roman candle, you know, Nod, like a Roman . . . with a candle, couple of rockets, Chinese fountain.

DON (in high-pitched childish voice) What does that do then?

NODDY (mimicking Don's childish voice) Yeah, what does that do then?

DON Hey, shut up or I'll give you one.

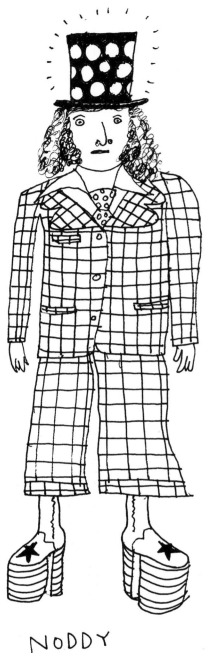

NODDY

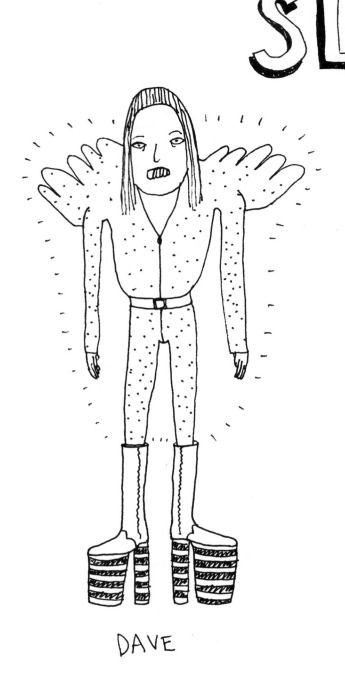

DAVE

JIM   I don't know really . . . I suppose it's just a little yellow squirt . . . *(pointing towards kitchen)*

JIM (cont)   Like Dave.

Enter Dave

DAVE   Hey, I hear that . . . look, Noddy, I'm not going to be able to shift anything with this muck . . . I mean, look at the ingredients . . . water . . .

NODDY   And . . .

DAVE   Nothing . . . that's it, just water . . . I need at least a lemon content . . . everyone knows you need lemon to shift ground-on dirt . . . it's no good unless I get some Lemon Fresh. You're going to have to have your Cup-A-Soup from paper cups.

NODDY, JIM AND DON   Oh no.

NODDY   I can't. I spent up buying this meat.

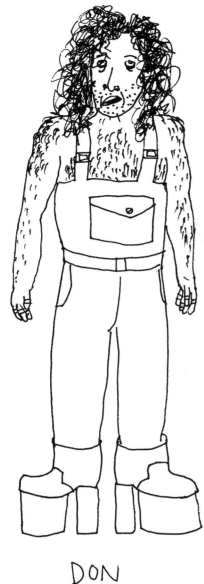

DON

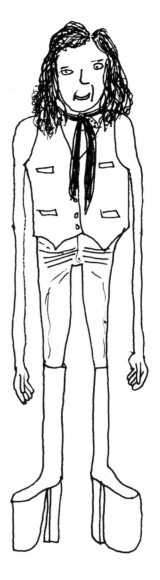

JIM

DAVE   You lot make me want to retch . . . and you . . . *(looking at Jim)*

DAVE (cont)   Don't count those fireworks in front of the fire . . . are you stupid as well as thick . . .?

Exit Dave.

DON   Jim, is there a Catherine wheel in the selection?

NODDY   Oh yeah, I love them . . . all sparkly and go round and round, lots and lots of colours flying out from a fixed point . . . round and round it goes . . . it sort of mesmerizes you and draws you in . . . it's like fairies twinkling and shimmering on your lawn . . . oh yeah, I love those Catherine wheels . . . is there one, Jim?

JIM   *(reading side of firework box)* No Catherine wheel included.

NODDY   Oh, that's just great, innit? . . . no, Catherine wheel and no clean cups.

A ring is heard from the front doorbell. Noddy answers the door. It is Roy Wood out of Wizzard dressed in his full battle dress.

NODDY   All right, Roy?

ROY   All right, Slade?

SLADE   All right, Roy?

ROY   Hey, fellas, look at this. I was down the shops in me bubble car and I got this new Lemon Fresh washing-up liquid, guaranteed to shift any stain . . . even red paint and guess what? . . . you get a free Catherine wheel with every bottle.

NODDY   Get down and get with it.

All of Slade administer a Slade point to Roy.

CUT TO   Vic and Bob.

WATER FIGHT

VIC   What's that on your face?

BOB   A little bit of blood.

VIC   Were you in a fight?

BOB   No it was a naughty cat.

VIC   Let's throw some water at each other.

BOB   Oh yes, let's.

As they sit down behind the desk they commence throwing numerous one-litre unopened bottles of either Evian or Volvic mineral water at each other.

VIC   This isn't much fun, this.

BOB   I know, let's get the hosepipes out.

Vic and Bob then produce a garden hosepipe each and point them at each other. We hear the sound of water rushing powerfully through the pipes. Vic and Bob gurgle in anticipation of the imminent torrent. When the water appears, however, it is one of the most pathetic trickles ever produced by Neptune. This, however, does not bother our two comedians as they whoop and holler as if under attack from Hollywood's celebrated Backdraft team . . . Interestingly, despite the pitiful trickle, there is a second effect that mimics the sound of two correctly working hosepipes.

BOB   I'm soaked.

Vic and Bob in extreme close-up laughing (see Shows One and Two).

VIC   Me too.

Vic and Bob in extreme close-up laughing. Up pops Greg Mitchell, the lovely cuddly doggy woggy.

GREG MITCHELL

GREG   Hello, Greg Mitchell. I enjoyed that water fight. Talking about water, I've just spend £350 on one of those new water filter jugs . . . Oh gawd, what have I done, my wife's going to kill me . . .

Up pops Greg's friend Corky.

CORKY   Water filter, Gregory, you want to treat your wife better, some champagne, some sovereign rings, some tickets for Upton Park to watch the Hammers.

GREG   I know, Corky, but I haven't got the money.

CORKY   You poncy git, Gregory. Come and do a job with me – I'll meet you at the lock up at 7 o'clock tonight.

GREG   Is it all above board?

CORKY   *(very faintly)* Of course it is Greg, my son, just you keep stumm.

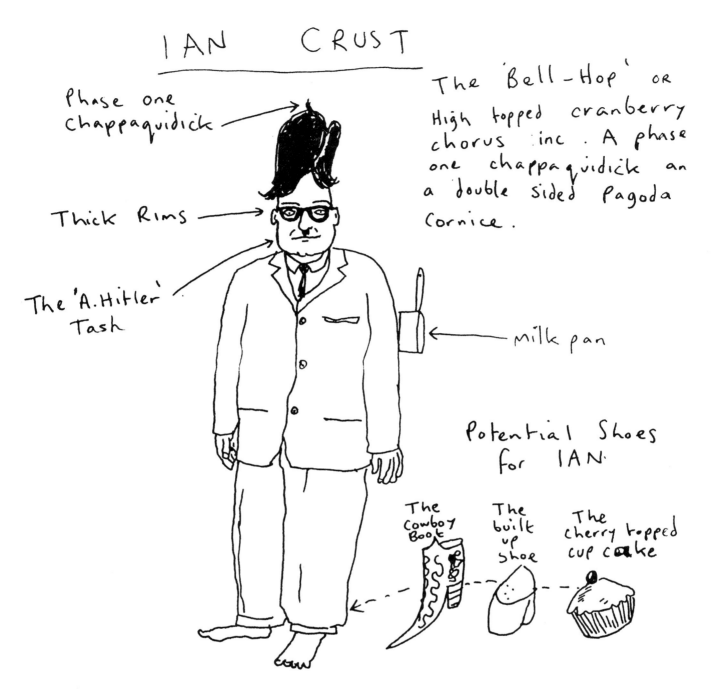

IAN CRUST

Phase one chappaquidick

Thick Rims

The 'A.Hitler' Tash

The 'Bell-Hop' or High topped cranberry chorus inc . A phase one chappaquidick an a double sided Pagoda Cornice.

milk pan

Potential Shoes for IAN.

The Cowboy Boot

The built up shoe

The cherry topped cup cake

CELEBRITY GUEST: IAN CRUST

Vic introduces this week's celebrity guest it is: Ian Crust, the inventor of the bag

VIC Evening, Mr Crust.

IAN Just call me Shorty.

VIC Why?

IAN Well, short crust . . . the pastry.

VIC Eh, I might as well call you Earth . . . like the earth crust.

IAN No, it's like pastry, you know.

VIC No I don't know, I might as well call you Pie Crust if pastry is your game.

IAN Look, it's not important. Can we just get on?

VIC OK. *(long pause)* Puff.

IAN Pardon?

VIC Puff . . . Puff pastry.

IAN Stop that.

VIC You started it, you puff.

IAN I'm not a puff!

VIC You are, it's obvious.

IAN I'm not. I'm a shorty.

VIC *(sternly)* All right, shortarse puff.

IAN *(getting up to leave)* I'm sorry. That's it, I'm leaving.

VIC I'm sorry. Sit down, you puff.

IAN *(sitting down then realizing)* I'm not a puff.

VIC I'm sorry, Puffy. Crusty . . . Shorty, yes, Shorty. Now, Parsley, you are the inventor of the bag.

Ian explains that he is indeed the inventor of the bag and spouts forth the following juvenile rant: first bag was seed pouch invented 1963; fisherman's cap made by filling the holes in his hairnet; oh mother of pearl I wouldn't change you for another girl, what you doing now, Roxy Music, oh Papa's got a brand new bag Papa Nicole Who? Nicole.

VIC Just tell us about the bags.

IAN Oh, all right then. I've brought along me latest bag.

VIC Well Shorty, let's have a look at it.

Cue opening bars of the closing song 'Let's Have a Look At It'.

Bob puts bag on desk. From this bag Vic and Bob pull out various items that help illustrate the words to the haunting song that follows:

SONG: 'LET'S HAVE A LOOK AT IT'

I love to look beneath a trout,
I like to obscure my vision with a used sprout,
Once again I have discovered nowt.

Chorus
Never mind, Vic, let's have a look at it,
That's right, Shorty, let's have a sniff of it,
Come along now, let's have a little bit more,
I love to examine deposits left by Jerry Hall,
I've further obscured my sight using a slide of
    Charles de Gaulle,
Sadly, Bob, once again I've discovered Nick all,
Come on now, let's have a look at it.
I can't, man, I'm temporarily blinded.
Well that's your lot then, we can't look at
    anything more.

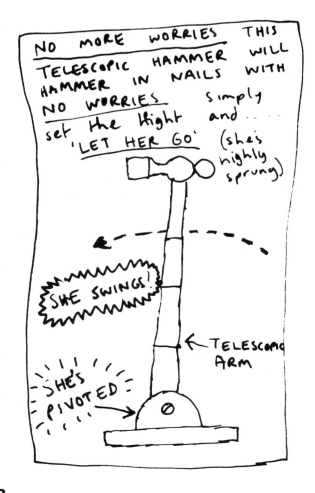

This here is Mr Mortimer (Mort) offering up an onion to mr Reeves (Reevo).

This here is Mick Box and Lee Kerslake the sailors. They, incidently, were also members of Uriah Heep.
(NICE ONE)

This here
is Eric Potter
and Jack Dent
wallpapering
a plough. →

This here is
Eric Potter & J.D.
pumping a dry
stone wall.

Eric Potter has
a Haemaglobin problem
where as J. Dent
has a urinary
disorder both of
which are receiving
treatment.

THE PASSAGE TO INDIA + THE CELTIC RANGER.

THE CORNBALL & THE STOOLPIGEON.

THE LARK ASCENDING.

THE QUININE REPORT.

This here is Mortimer with his over large bumbag which he is rather sensitive about.

This bloke here has an inflamed colon but he's getting treatment so don't worry.

Mr Reeves here is thinking about buying a cordless kettle ——→

This here is ————————→ Susan Mitchell
Greg's second wife, his first was Sondra
(like Sondra
lock. Clint's
first wife)
She died,
sadly from
a 'cronic'
arthritis.

This here is Noddy Hodler out
of SLADE (The group).

This here is D. Hill announcing that there
is no Lemon content in the washing up
Liquid (Bad Luck D. Hill!)

NICE ONE.

This here is Dent & Potter doing earpiercing.

Here they are in the WOODS!

This here is them
on their underfloor
Return of the Jedi
Badge.
They also own an
underfloor mouse-sized
gymnasium £4.40 a look.

OH NO! IT'S MR POTTY!

Here R&M offer their condolences to some Joker in the crew backed up by some Pom Pom girls.

This here is Mr Reeves with a gun in Mr Mortimer's back insisting he finish the song.

THIS IS
ONE HECK
OF A CHEESE
(as it is
'walk me Home'
cheddar)

Mrs R & M
seem very
contented
with the
info they
have been
given by
Otis & Marvin
don't they?

(Yes!)

This Here Is
Mulligan & O'Hare
on their style.

(MULLIGAN & O'HARE)

Here they have G.Deperdieu
obscuring their view of each
other.

This here is plate Fungus being displayed
by Mr Mulligan. Mr O'Hare is up the tree
They both suffer from burst urethas and
peppered glands but they're having them seen
to — so dont fret!

DAVE HILL

NODDY   &   DAVE

SHOW

OPENING TITLES

Well here we are, and we're all acutely aware of dramatic climatical changes in England and the associated stress this causes in people's inadequately ventilated homes.

Musical instruments, e.g. the guitar, violin, flute, double bass and triangle have always been correctly ventilated with holes and slits and that. Having said that, tools such as the hammer, saw, screwdriver, set square and grousemandle have, like our homes, suffered from severe underventilation.

It is not as if products are not available to create a properly ventilated environment, i.e. the hole; the slit; the gap; and of course the vent axia, the expelair, the duct ex and the air conditioning unit.

Literally millions of pounds are wasted every year eradicating from the home the symptoms of inadequate ventilation such as dampness, hard vegetables, warts, carpet dryness, dust in tankard, moistness in your Frosties, shower curtain speckling, drunkenness in billiard room and the biggest waste of all, rust on your flat barrow.

Surely this money could be better spent properly ventilating the home and using the saved monies to explore new worlds beyond our sun or installing concealed lighting in all homes, not just those of the rich and famous.

It's worth thinking about . . . isn't it?

So let's make a start by making this show a ventilation and air conditioning special.

VOICE-OVER Ladies and gentlemen, unblock your airbricks, ventilate your roof space and say farewell to foist in your home with Britain's most carefree indoor climate control engineers and choreographers . . . Reeves and Mortimer!

Enter Vic and Bob along with three male and three female dancers. These dancers are professional Equity card holding, light entertainment dancers. They are not the street cred, cycling short mob that you get parading about on Dance Energy *or behind Kylie. They are simply young, keen, attractive dancers who would be perfect on* Sunday Night at the Palladium *July 1993. We do not wish to get any joke out of the appearance of these dancers . . . They will, however, be required to perform some unusual dancing.*

For the first few lines of the following song, Vic and Bob and dancers are in perfect harmony as they perform a tightly choreographed dance routine. The dancers then peel off leaving Vic and Bob to demonstrate their air conditioning and continue to dance in the background of the two air conditioning obsessed comic actors. Their dance routine includes the following ideas expressed as movement:

- *A man controlling a wild stallion*
- *A telephone receptionist operating her controls with her elbow*
- *Gene Autrey trying to pick a lock on a moving bread-van (in Hull)*
- *A man walking through tar to accept a free hairdrier from Daryl Hannah*
- *A telephone ringing at Mrs Bridges' tea shop*
- *A man repeatedly grabbing at a cactus whilst sipping on a nice claret.*

SONG: 'COOL CONDITIONED AIR'

I thought I had the perfect home,
I had my cavity walls filled with foam,
central heating on full,
my roof full of wool,
but I still got dampness on my walls walls walls walls.

My lettuce was starting to curl,
I had dampness in my world,
the kids were crying,
my clothes weren't drying,
and my shower curtain was covered in spores
    spores spores spores.

Chorus
We needed cool cool conditioned air,
feel it flowing through one's hair,
under your chair and everywhere,
cool cool air.

Spoken
That was until the 23rd of July, when we installed
the following indoor climate control systems into
our dockside Portsmouth flat.

NB *The following items are available on stage for*
Vic and Bob to demonstrate: a dehumidifier, an
ioniser air purifier.

Don't forget the horsedrawn hairdrier,
The Who live at Leeds, a packet of seeds,
And a top hat full of Gloy Gloy Gloy Gloy.

Chorus

For the final chorus the dancers return to centre
stage to dance with the comic actors. The final
refrain of 'Cool Cool Air' is repeated over and
over again. The vocals are lowered as the dancers
themselves do the dance of the child criminals in
West Side Story you know the one where
Georgiou Limon Caracou and his co-star Gwen
Furlong crouch as if they have been kicked in the
guts (stomach) but still insist on clicking their fat
little fingers). They leap up and the music reaches
a climax for a final celebatory thanksgiving to the
gift of cool air in the living room.

Vic and Bob and dancers remain standing in a
line all breathing very heavily out of exhaustion
and smiling at the camera through their obvious
discomfort.

The camera noses about in close-up amongst the

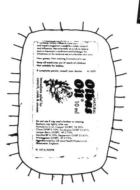

Please read Directions and Ingredients
in order to establish the correct length
of time that a camera must linger
on panting dancers (post to churchill when
used)

faces of the exhausted dancers. Their breathing is
very loud. These are uncomfortable shots and the
camera stays on the dancers for the time it would
take to read out loud the directions for use and
ingredients on a bottle of Olbas Oil (see
drawing).

(NB *A potential funny gag here would be to have*
a 'pantometer' at the bottom of the screen which
indicates the level of panting by use of
thermometer liquid passing through hearts and
lighting them up, i.e. as the panting increases the
liquid rises.)

Exit dancers taking with them the air
conditioning products prayed to above.

VIC & BOB

Vic and Bob 'curn' to their desk and greet the
audience with a rousting mult. As they are doing
so a royal blue Ford Escort van (not nice new one,
no, a bit rough) speeds on to the stage and
screeches to a halt. The back doors of the van
burst open and a big cuddly duck is thrown out

on to the stage floor. The van then immediately screeches off stage.

The aston 'action replay' is flashed on the screen. We see the whole van incident again but this time in slow motion and featuring Vic and Bob making very silly faces and distinctive hand movements at the desk . . . You see it isn't an action replay at all!

At the desk:

VIC Did you spot the difference?

Vic and Bob discuss air conditioning using the worded script that you, the reader, can find right at the beginning of this script.

VIC The opening song was good but the old songs are the best, aren't they, Bob?

BOB Yeah, like what?

VIC (in form of Latin chant) Non est factum José Carreras.

BOB Oh yes, that's a lovely ditty.

There now follows a series of very poor quickfire jokes. It must be appreciated that the jokes themselves are appalling, in fact, at the end of the day, they are not even jokes. Anyhow, that's not the point, see, copper, 'cos it's like this, see: immediately after each joke is delivered Vic and Bob employ a selection from the following demonstrations of approval:

1 A private honk on the personal car horn of the teller

2 The phrases 'that's very funny', 'don't don't', 'you like that one, listen to this', 'get out of here'

3 A dig on a receptionist's buzzer

4 A good hearty stir of some cake mix in a brown mixing bowl

5 Cleansing stainless steel hospital vomiting dish

6 Someone's head pops up from behind desk and it is shampooed rapidly

7 Same head pops up and is rinsed rapidly.

BOB I went to Leicester the other day.

VIC Oh yeah?

BOB Yeah, I'm not going there again.

Ha ha ha ha ha ha ha ha, etc.

VIC A friend of mine works as a swimming pool attendant.

BOB Oh yeah, does he enjoy it?

VIC Not any more, he got the sack.

Heehee hee hee hee ho ho ho ho.

A man's head pops up through trap door on desk covered in foamy shampoo. Bob shampoos his hair – he pops down again.

BOB I phoned the fire brigade yesterday.

VIC Was your house on fire?

BOB No, actually I dialled the wrong number.

VIC I went to the doctor's the other day.

BOB Really, what did he prescribe?

VIC A hair net.

Following this last joke, the man whose hair has been washed gets out from behind the desk, puts his trilby hat back on and exits.

BOB (seriously) Well, that's been a bit of fun, but there was actually something on a more serious note that we'd like you to see . . . so if you're ready, Vic . . .

Vic and Bob then commence pulling piggy, funny faces to camera and audience saying:

VIC AND BOB Look, look at me . . . see this now.

REEVES AND MORTIMER PRODUCTS FACTORY TOUR

Vic and Bob are in the studio.

BOB   A lot of people write asking if they can visit the Reeves and Mortimer secret factory at Unit 4, Chappeldale Industrial Estate, Whitstable . . . wait for it . . . Kent.

VIC   Well, obviously we can't do that as the location of the factory must remain *(holding up file with the words 'top secret' written on it)* top secret.

BOB   But what we have done is made our own documentary.

VIC   *(butting in)* . . . film.

BOB   Yeah, all right, documentary film.

VIC   *(speaking at the same time as Bob)* Documentary film.

BOB   Look, pack it in. Who's doing this?

VIC   You are.

BOB   Right, well, shut up . . . so what we have done is made our own documentary film . . .

VIC   *(interrupting)* presentation.

BOB   Right, you do it.

VIC   OK, will do . . . so what we have done is made our own documentary film presentation entitled *One Man's Genius*.

BOB   Eh . . . one man's genius.

CUT TO   Opening shot of One Man's Genius.

First shot is of large double industrial estate type doors with 'Unit Four' written on them.

Off camera we hear:

BOB   We're here at . . .

VIC   *(interrupting)* Hold on, what do you think you're doing? . . . I'm doing the talking.

BOB   Well, does it matter?

VIC   Yes, it does . . . you're just trying to sneak in whilst I set up the shot.

BOB   Oh, shut it . . . *(Bob walks into shot)* . . . We're here at the . . .

Vic   *(off camera interrupting)* Action!

BOB   We're here at the . . .

VIC   *(off camera interrupting)* Cut!

BOB   *(looking round camera straight at Vic)* What's all this action cut cut action? Who do you think you are . . . the Warner Brothers? Look, turn that off.

Screen goes dark for four seconds. Then there is the image you get when a video is pulling into focus. It focuses in on the following image . . .

Vic is now standing in front of the Unit Four gate. It is a full-length shot. Vic is wearing a light blue cotton safari suit with the collars of a cream silk shirt (large pointed collars) over the collar of the safari suit. The trousers are slightly too short, revealing plain white towelling socks bubbling over the lips of a pair of Nigerian car shoes.

He has had his hair heavily bouffed and has clearly put too much foundation make-up on . . .

BOB   *(quietly into camera microphone)* What does he look like . . . Action!

Vic very slowly turns his head to camera and gives one of the most flamboyant and irrational looks to camera that any one man could ever give.

BOB   Cut! . . . Vic, get on with it . . . Action!

Vic again performs his magical look to camera and then says in the voice of a fool . . .

VIC Hi . . . (*waving hand and turning to door*) . . . this is where dreams can come true . . .

BOB (*off camera interrupting*) Oh God, that's it, let's just get inside . . . Cut!

Camera is turned off.

CUT TO   Inside of factory. Bob is beside a workbench. Sat behind the workbench is Uncle Peter. He is wearing a brown laboratory type workman's coat with an R&M motif on breast pocket.

On the bench is the Reeves and Mortimer will duplicating sink . . . Vic is operating camera. The above image comes into view.

VIC Action!

BOB Well, here we are inside the factory on one of the production lines . . .

VIC (*interrupting*) Cut!

BOB What's the problem now?

VIC Make-up!

BOB Look, it's just me and you. We haven't got a make-up artist . . . (*Looks to camera, nodding as if to say 'come on move it, acknowledge the correctness of my last statement.'*)

VIC (*after short pause*) I'll do it for you.

Camera off and then back on again to reveal Bob in position as before, but now sporting heavily mascaraed eyes and eyebrows.

VIC Action!

BOB Well, here we are inside the factory on one of the production lines. Here is a face you'll be familiar with, our Uncle Peter who's been working with us here in the factory for over twenty years. Uncle Peter, what are you working on today?

At this point Bob turns full face on to camera and delivers an insincere smile, revealing the full hideousness of his appearance . . . This causes Vic to commence muffled giggling from behind the camera. Bob responds to this with a single sharp look.

PETER It's the will duplicating sink.

BOB Sorry . . . the?

PETER The Reeves and Mortimer will duplicating sink.

BOB Well, that sounds self-explanatory. Can we actually see it in action?

At this point Vic appears next to Bob holding an aluminium stem with legs, i.e. the sort of thing that would hold a light in the air . . . only the stem is seen, not the light at the top.

BOB Hold on, Peter . . . (*to Vic*) What are you doing?

VIC Fixing up some proper lights.

BOB Well, who's looking after the camera?

VIC Look, I know what I'm doing . . . it's on a tripod . . . you do your job and I'll do mine.

BOB So, as I was saying, Peter, that sounds quite self-explanatory. Could we see it in action?

As Bob is delivering the above lines, the camera has begun to slowly sink towards the ground. This means that by the time Bob commences the following explanation, he is no longer in view . . .

We hear a machine click into action.

BOB As you can see, the sink is initially filled with literally thousands of gallons of PLJ, the acidic lemon drink, direct from what we believe to be Camelot, via this faulty Tudor conduit. The will to be copied is then placed into this model paddle steamer where it is painstakingly copied by this two-hundred-weight, luminous, whistling canary . . .

Sound effects to accompany the above as follows:

- Sound of gushing acidic lemon drink
- Sound of paddle steamer hoot hoot ding a ling incorporating honky tonk piano
- Sound of whistling canary just prior to it infusing poisoned gas

Now during the above speech the camera has fallen to the floor and then been slowly raised up again by Vic (whom we may have heard exclaim 'Oh shit,' or something similar when the camera reached the bottom of its descent). This means that by the time Bob delivers the following line, he is back in view . . .

BOB   (holding successfully duplicated will in hand which simply reads, 'I, William Tate, bequeath all my wordly goods to Messrs Reeves and Mortimer, unit four, etc. etc.) Producing this perfectly duplicated will.

VIC   Lights!

At this point the scene is assaulted by some of the most poweful tungsten megawatt fluoride light one can imagine.

BOB   Aaaaaaargh . . . turn it off, I'm burning!

VIC   You're too hot? . . . Hold on.

Vic then turns on a 2000 mega breeze wind machine that causes many items to blow into the picture including:

- another worker
- a couple of stuffed dogs
- Mr Porridge
- a harp
- a bra that gets trapped on Bob's face

Bob, still screaming, reaches towards camera, knocking it down and it goes dead.

CUT TO   Vic and Bob are standing either side of a serving hatch in the middle of a wall, i.e. not part of a canteen or anything. Above the hatch are the words R&M canteen. On the foldback door is printed the following menu . . .

MENU 1993

Starters	Main Courses
Biscuits 80p	Shallow fried grouse:
Fat £1.80	whole £22.50
Top of the milk 25p	half £22.42
Mini bites 50p	Many mini bites £1.00
	Ronnie's Pot £POA

All main courses are served with thick sauce, thin sauce, juice, button mushrooms, crisps and a whole roast chicken.

Puddings	Beverages (Drinks)
Hand-varnished pears	Top of the milk 24p
72p each	Wine drink
Whelks in hot tap water	(bottle) £2.40
£1.00 each	(cup) 80p
Hot vinegar cup 5p	

Extras

Towel   35p

VIC   Are you all right, Peter? . . . Sure you can manage?

PETER   (for it is he behind the camera) Action!

BOB   (who is now bright orange on one side due to burning and whose eye mascara has been blown into many spidery streams as has his hair) Hello again. Here we are the workers' canteen looking at some of the items on the 1993 menu.

VIC   That's right. You might like to try one of our starters . . . er, perhaps the mini bites and for the main course a whole shallow fried grouse for £22.50 or perhaps just a half for a very reasonable £22.42. All main courses are served with thick sauce, thin sauce and, of course, a whole roast chicken.

BOB   If you're still hungry after that, which I much doubt, what about a hand-varnished pear, or if you're doing very repetitive work, the hot vinegar cup. Wash the lot down with one of our selection of beverages.

VIC   Drinks.

BOB   It's the same thing.

VIC   Is it? . . . Carry on.

BOB   Such as the wine style drink . . . Ah, look, here comes one of the workers now to place his order . . .

Vic motions to Uncle Peter to get out from behind the camera and pretend to be the customer . . . camera shakes slightly and Uncle Peter emerges from behind camera and approaches hatch as Vic and Bob move purposefully out of frame.

PETER   A bowl of Ronnie's Pot, please.

From behind counter, up pops a male human arse with an eye drawn on each arse cheek.

Cut as camera goes off.

Camera goes back on. We are outside again in front of the unit four factory doors.

Bob is standing outside the Unit Four door.

BOB   Well, we hope you've enjoyed your visit to the Reeves and Mortimer secret factory here at Unit Four.

VIC   *(from behind camera)* Oh shit!

We then hear the sound of running footsteps which represent the sound of Vic fleeing the scene using his footsteps to do so.

BOB   Hey, where do you think you're going?

At this point, Bob's attention is diverted to a large man in a padded anorak with wide hair and a hand-held microphone. He is facing Bob and is therefore seen from behind.

Bob looks sheepish.

MAN   Hello, Mr Mortimer, I'm Roger Cook from Central Television and I'd like to ask you about a will duplicating scam that you and your partner, Mr Reeves, who I might add is an illegal immigrant, are operating from these premises.

LOOK

CHOCOLATE

THE CAT BURGLARS STANCE

Running footsteps are once again heard as Vic returns to the scene.

BOB   Oh, you're back, are you?

VIC   Yeah, hang on, I'll deal with this.

COOK   What the . . .

You see, what has happened is that Vic has picked up camera and tripod, held it high in the air and brought it sharply down on to the fat smug face of Roger Cook, thus leaving us with the final image of a terrified Cook saying, 'What the – aaarrrggghhh?'

Camera to darkness.

VIC   Cut!

BOB   Yes, quite badly too.

CUT TO   We are back in the studio and Vic and Bob are standing centre stage mimicking the stance that a cat burglar might use if he were startled mid cat burgle. They either have their pants round their ankles or are bare chested. They have an amount of chocolate around their mouths both of which are situated on their faces (see drawing).

Vic is staring directly into the camera, Bob is staring sideways in the Abbaresque manner. Their voices are in the manner of early BBC radio presenters like Leslie Winters or Ken Hill, or the beautiful rolling Sussex Downs, or Suffolk, or a young girl holding a daisy chain up towards that giant thing, you know, Frankenstein and the mummy's curse bloke.

VIC   That was a message from the British Information Board.

BOB   And, now, live from the Pease Pudding Marketing Board . . .

VIC   In a joint presentation with the Toffee Information Desk . . . It's the Uncle Peter Band . . .

CUT TO   Pre-recorded performance by the Uncle Peter Band. Set as per usual with the addition of the Timotei lass in her chair as the audience.

UNCLE PETER BAND

PETER   I'd walk a million miles
over broken glass
if you would say to me
that you would be my lass.

VIC & BOB   Yes, Peter, yes
That's what you must do now.

PETER   Ey!

End of song

PETER   I didn't mean it . . . I'll tell you that.

At this point Peter begins to smash up his drumkit. Final shot is of girlfriend looking like a shy and coy Victorian girl who has been surprised to find the butler showing her his arse. She is clutching a nice bunch of daffs with a label attached to them saying 'From Uncle Peter'.

NB It hasn't been mentioned, like, but the actress who plays the part of the Timotei girl must be very tall indeed and quite thick-set, like, but not fat. Sorry, we didn't mention this earlier only, like, you know, we forgot, you know, and that's how it goes like, you know, when you're busy and that, like, so don't start saying 'owt, like, 'cos what's the point, like . . . you know.

VIC AND BOB: BRITISH AIRFIELD

CUT TO   Vic and Bob at desk. They are unaware that the camera has returned to the studio and are busy reading their respective newspapers.

BOB   What page is your TV guide on, Vic?

VIC   Five.

BOB   *(slightly worried)* Mine's on nine . . . What times does yours say that *Playbox* starts?

VIX   Er, 12.10.

BOB   *(relieved)* Oh that's all right then, they're the same.

VIC   *(reading from the paper)* Ah, 9 o'clock *The Way To the Stars* starring Michael Redgrave ner ner ner ner ner ner ner ner British airfield . . . That doesn't sound very good.

BOB   What was that bit in the middle?

VIC   Ner ner ner ner ner ner ner ner . . .

BOB   That sounds useless.

VIC   Well what does it say in yours?

BOB   *The Way To the Stars* starring Michael Redgrave ner ner ner ner ner ner ner ner British airfield.

VIC   It doesn't sound so bad in your paper.

BOB   Non non, Pierre, it sounds all right.

NB *The following dialogue is a pre-recorded mind-thought section where the audience and viewers are encouraged to believe that they can hear Vic and Bob's thoughts.*

VIC   Oh great, 3.30 *Learning to Swim* – that's my favourite.

BOB   Brilliant, 3.30 *Fraggle Rock* – I bloody love that show.

VIC   Oh no, it clashes with *Fraggle* bloody *Rock* . . . He's not going to let me watch it.

BOB   *(singing)* Down at Fraggle Rock toot toot . . . I can't wait . . . Oh, it clashes with that *Learn to Swim* . . . well, he's not watching it.

VIC   Him and his bloody *Fraggle Rock* toot toot. I'm never going to learn to swim at this rate . . . I only saw the first one and that just showed me how to get me trunks on . . . It's all right for him, he never goes near water.

End of mind-thought.

BOB   What do you mean I never go near water. Are you suggesting something?

VIC   Yes I am. You never wash, you stink . . . Everyone on the estate knows . . . Why do you think no one bothers to visit us any more?

BOB   I'll tell you why no one visits . . . It's because you prance about in your swimming trunks telling everyone you can swim . . . Everyone on the estate knows you can't . . . Why do you think we're barred from the swimming baths?

VIC   I'll tell you why . . . it's because the last time we went you turned up dressed as Gobi out of *Fraggle Rock* and blocked up the filter system with your harp.

BOB   Ah, so you admit I have had a wash.

VIC   Once!

At this point the argument is interrupted by Uncle Peter, who is standing next to the previously discarded duck in the company of his suspected girlfriend. The duck has rope entwined around its body.

UNCLE PETER   Here, kitty kitty . . . get off my land! . . . *(turning to girlfriend)* I own this land as far as the eye can see . . . It could be yours one day if you play your cards right . . . *(turning back to duck)* Get off my land!

BOB   *(leaning down to stare wantonly into the eyes of the duck)* Oh isn't she a beauty . . . Ah, I could eat you all up.

VIC   *(pathetically tucking in behind Bob and trying to get a decent view)* Yeah, me too.

At this point the perspective of the camera switches to that of the duck (a fish-eye lens). The duck is seeing Vic, Bob, Peter and the Timotei girl all shifting about in front of its face to adore it.

VIC   *(voice fading to assist switch to duck's viewpoint)* Oh, I'd like to wrap you up and take you home with me.

Now the duck speaks and everyone is going to be surprised to find that it speaks with the voice of a 57-year-old West Indian Lady called Beatrice. Throughout Beatrice's words Vic, Bob et al., are seen vying for the best position to look deeply into the duck's eyes.

DUCK   What a day I be having now. Let me tell you I went down to the bank to make a lickle withdrawal, then two boys step forward all of a sudden and do overpower me. I get kidnapped and taken a hostage and lord what sort of a damn fool place is this to bring me with these boys touching me and a staring at me like I was the whore of Babylon, you ras clarts.

At this point the perspective of the camera returns to outside the duck.

BOB   Oh, you're the loveliest cuddly wuddly duck in the land.

Fading as camera moves over to desk where Greg Mitchell is about to pop up.

GREG MITCHELL

GREG   *(already in position behind desk)* Hello, Greg Mitchell here. See that duck down there . . . well me and Corky kidnapped her this morning during a bank raid we carried out to raise cash for me to take the wife to see the Dave Lee Travis Roadshow . . . Unfortunately Corky dumped me and the duck here and cleared off with all the money . . . My wife's going to kill me . . .

At this point the Ford Escort van arrives and screeches to a holt (not halt spelt rongly). We see the driver's window round down (not wound spelt rongly), (you don't have to be made to work here, but it helps) revealing that the driver is Corky Thompson, Greg's best friend.

CORKY   Gregory, shut it! You want to get us banged up? I wouldn't stitch you up, my son. I had to drop the wedge at the lock-up. Now get that bleeding hostage in here and let's get out of it!

We see Gregory drop down behind the desk. A modern camera angle is then employed to show Greg walking across the stage to the motor. The viewer would see Gregory from the chest up and, most importantly, would see him putting on his trilby. And just as importantly there would be a close-up of his feet walking, wearing a pair of black buckled and winkled goth-style shoes. About as important is a brief shot of Greg, apparently putting the duck into the back of the van.

VOICE-OVER   Come on, Gregory, get in the Jag. This place is crawling with filth.

Close-up shot of the back door of van closing and van screeching off again out of the studio.

AND SO ENDS THIS LITTLE SNIPPET OF
LIFE IN LONDON

MULLIGAN AND O'HARE

Mulligan and O'Hare haredrift on to stage with their hands behind their backs with short sting from 'My Rose Has Left Me'.

VIC   Hello, ladies and gentlemen my name is Dermott Mulligan.

BOB   And my name is Dermott O'Hare.

VIC   We are halfway through our British tour which started yesterday at Leicester Forest East service station.

BOB   And finishes tomorrow at the Harlequin Shopping Centre in Thanet.

VIC   You boy sit down, yes you with the face of a pig, sit down.

BOB   Tonight we would like to sing a song about my wife Rose. Now Rose and I met in a hospital in Swansea when I was having a few adjustments made to my new leg.

VIC   Yes, Rose was having surgery to remove a tattoo of St Paul from her back and to dislodge an old ankle chain that her calf skin had grown over.

BOB   Unfortunately this surgery left her bald . . .

VIC   . . . In every department.

BOB   After hospital we moved to a hostel and it was there in the communal washroom that we first held hands.

VIC   Yes, you were drawn to her by the smell of the dermatological cream that she was washing off her toupee. We then purchased a caravan using the compensation money O'Hare received for the loss of his leg.

BOB   Yes it was about this time that Mulligan became addicted to Rose's hormone tablets and became subject to violent mood swings.

VIC   Anyway Rose eventually left us for a bloke from Allied Carpets and neither of them have been seen for six weeks.

BOB   But I assure you we both have alibis . . . I was at Mulligans that night.

VIC   And I was at O'Hare's.

BOB   Anyway this song is dedicated to the memory of our Rose.

'My Rose Has Left Me'.

My Rose has left me,
I'm in a mood,
She went to Kenya,
With the bloke from Allied Carpets.

She couldn't have children.
That didn't stop us from trying,
We were turned down for adoption
Due to her bizarre appearance.
Oh Rose how we loved you
But where are you now?

Alone with your salesman you adulterous cow.

They bow and say goodnight.

OTIS & MARVIN WITH SPECIAL GUEST ROSE MARIE

UNCLE PETER   You two could have helped the little duck . . . you're useless . . . you just stood there like two monkeys.

VIC   It's usually donkeys with you, innit, Peter?

PETER   Donkey! . . . donkey! Ee-haw . . . monkey . . . uh uh uh . . . *(Peter begins to leave stage, as he does so saying)* duck . . . quack . . . dog . . . woof bark I'll tell you that! . . . monkeys.

BOB   He's right, you know, we probably should have helped.

VIC   Hmmmm, maybe, Bob, but it's funny because I didn't actually see anything . . . in fact, although I have perfect sight, I've never seen anything apart from, of course, sounds.

BOB   Mmm, that's interesting, Vic, because although my eyesight is considered nearly perfect, I don't actually have the ability to look . . . in fact, I've never looked at anything in my life apart, of course, from the occasional mist.

VIC   Mmm, that makes sense Bob because, of course, you were born without looks . . .

BOB   *(smiling)* I'll pretend I didn't hear that.

VIC   It's difficult though, Bob . . . I mean, should you assist when you see a crime being committed or just walk on by?

BOB   I know, Vic, let's ask Otis and Marvin . . . they are over there.

VIC   Bob, how quick you forget . . . I can't actually see . . .

BOB   Oh, don't start that again.

We then hear the muffled sound of Otis, Marvin and a girl having an altercation . . . it is clearly coming from within the monitor in which they choose to live.

Vic and Bob indicate to each other visually to keep quiet and sneak over to the monitor and open the doors in such a way to clearly suggest they are going to be nosy parkers and eavesdrop on the argument.

CUT TO   Otis, Marvin and Rose Marie all sat on the dock of the bay as per usual.

MARVIN   But, Otis, she's not like the usual girls you pick up at the grapevine . . .

OTIS   *(interrupting)* Marvin, Marvin, Marvin, be quiet . . . you are becoming increasingly more mysterious in your behaviour . . . you know girls are not allowed on the dock to watch the ships coming in . . .

MARVIN   I know and going out again . . . but you don't understand. This is Rose Marie, the pretty singer from Ireland.

OTIS   I don't care if it's Diana Ross. THERE ARE NO GIRLS ALLOWED ON THE DOCK!

ROSE   Would you listen to that man . . . no girls on the dock indeed . . . I'm always here at the dockside waiting on the ships coming in.

OTIS   *(under breath)* You're not so interested when they're going out, though, are you?

ROSE   I'll pretend I didn't hear that!

MARVIN   Otis! Really . . . take no notice of him, come on and have a cuddle.

Marvin and Rose put their arms around each other and commence canoodling.

OTIS   *(clearly put out and mumbling, or perhaps muttering, definitely not whispering . . . that would be quite wrong . . . grumbling would be nearly right . . . but a growl is quite out of the question . . . hushed burbling mmmmmmmm . . . No, it wouldn't work . . .)* Honestly, you come here, you know, to watch ships coming in . . . and it's more like lovers' bloody lane with these two . . . where's my sandwiches? *(looking at watch)* Oh great, that consignment of kedgeree is due any minute now . . .

During the above, Rose and Marvin have been increasingly vocal in their courting, saying the following . . .

Illooooooooooo looooo lavvvvy lavvvvvy ooooooooocchi ooochi oooooo

i.e. lovey dovey mumblings.

Whilst these mumblings are being employed, Marvin's false arm and hand have been slowly moving down the length of Rose's dress. When he gets to the hem, he begins to lift it up . . . this causes fright in Rose and she says . . .

ROSE   Oh, you're like an octopus, Marvin Gaye, so you are.

This outburst is the final straw for Otis . . .

OTIS   Oh, Marvin man, you are becoming increasingly continental in your outlook . . . now either settle down and watch the ships coming in or clear off and leave me alone.

MARVIN   Oh, pardon me for breathing.

Otis begins concentrating intently on the horizon. Marvin turns to Rose and whispers something in her ear.

ROSE   Oh, Otis, OH, OTIS!

OTIS   Yes.

ROSE   How many ships have you got in your little book this month?

OTIS   *(embarrassed and under breath)* None.

ROSE   How many?

OTIS   NONE!

Marvin and Rose laugh and then Marvin again whispers into Rose's ear.

ROSE   Otis, oh, Otis.

OTIS   What now?

ROSE   Do you prefer to see the ships when they're coming in or going out?

Marvin sniggers under his hand.

OTIS   Well, now I'm often asked that . . .

ROSE   I bet you are *(sniggers under hand).*

OTIS   Well, it's nice when a ship comes in 'cos I always miss a beat when I get my first sighting . . . but, having said that, when I wave one goodbye as it goes out again, I do feel a certain pride . . .

At this point Marvin and Rose enter a fit of hysterical laughter.

OTIS   That's it . . . ha, ha, ha, it's very funny, isn't it? Are you staying here with me or going off with her?

MARVIN   Look, I'm sorry, Rose, but we are expecting a shipment of kedgeree to arrive any minute . . . so I think I'll stay here with Otis if you don't mind . . .

OTIS   *(interrupting excitedly)* Marvin, here it is now!

ROSE   Oh, bejabers, so it is . . . I'd better get a move on.

Rose quickly exits.

OTIS   Well, Marvin, I don't think you'll be seeing her again . . . at least not until that ship goes out.

At this point cut back to Vic and Bob stood watching the monitor.

VIC   Well, we're not going to get any sense out of them. Let's see what else is on.

Vic turns knob on television and it changes from Otis and Marvin to . . . A white psyche with a middle-aged man in green tights with a heavily padded arse and bare chest and wild red hair with a bottle of cider in his hand, stumbling about on account of being very, very drunk (Vic).

BOB   That doesn't look very interesting.

Bob turns channel and, hey presto, it is the beginning of Noel's addicts.

VIC   Ah, now that is more like it.

NOEL'S ADDICTS

This is a pre-recorded insert in which the comedians and some of their friends pretend they are presenting an episode of the popular weekend light entertainment programme that illustrates the loneliness in people's lives by displaying them alongside their tawdry little collections of thimbles, badges, underpants and the like in their putrid, damp and under-ventilated little hovels in dreadful little soulless northern towns such as Bath, Salisbury and Canterbury.

Holding the show together is the genial host Mr Noel Edmonds, a lovely bearded ex DJ. Now what Noel hates more than anything else is to be shown old photographs of himself from his radio days where he looks very similar to how he looks now except his shirt collars are slightly larger, his hair slightly less bleached and no jumper was required.

On the other hand, Noel just loves to be startled by an unnecessary and uncalled-for appearance by his old DJ chum 'the hairy cornflake' Dave Lee Travis (who interestingly also despises having old photographs of himself exhibited on the TV screen from his DJ days when he looked identical apart from slightly fewer grey hairs). Above all,

NOEL

ROLL OVER BEET HOVEN

ALL OVER FLESH COLOURED BODY STOCKING

NO WORRIES

KEEP ON TRUCKIN'

BLUE & WHITE 'COW' BOY BOOTS

everyone associated with the show loves fun, surprised pensioners, clever wordplay and koi carp. So here it is . . . *Noel's Addicts.*

Titles

Photograph of Noel, his eyes revolving as he stares at three doughnuts that are dancing above his head.

NOEL *(in the voice of a German who has been taught English by an American)* Von doo tree doughnuts. *(Noel licks his lips and the words 'Noel's Addicts' appear.)*

VOICE-OVER It's no no no no no noe noe Noel's Addicts. *(This is done verbally and not with the use of a sampler.)*

Set

It's just one of those sets that they have, or whatever they can afford, or if there's owt lying

about, or if one of the chippies could knock something up out of old wood – but if not it doesn't really matter.

The Show

Noel enters the set wearing his wig (see drawing) and wearing a complete body stocking i.e. flesh-coloured with chest hair, etc. This garment is heavily noduled with towels, vegetables, bottles, etc. It's a home-made affair that need not be subject to heavy thought or expense. An example of how it might look post-noduling is enclosed herewith.

PS *Every participant in this show is holding a vinegar bottle where possible.*

NOEL *(Bob)* Welcome to the wonderful world of addiction *(holds up a bottle of cider)*. Now everyone enjoys drinking cider, but you wouldn't want to drink this one *(turning bottle to reveal that it has a tiny fluorescent Wunderfulbra suspended within it)*, as it's got a tiny fluorescent Wunderfulbra suspended in it . . . Now all will become clear when I introduce you to my first guest Ken Taylor who has a collection of things suspended in bottles of cider. *(Noel walks over to area where Ken is situated. This area consists of a 2-foot square pine, school-type table with grey tubular metal legs. On the table are three bottles of cider, a half-eaten salami and a Brie French baguette sandwich and an old axe. Next to the table is Ken who is sat on a wooden schoolchair in the same style as the table. He is eating a slice of Mr Kipling's chocolate fudge cake on a white paper plate.)* Hello, Ken, nice to meet you.

KEN Yes, Noel, it's nice to meet you.

NOEL So, Ken, you suspend things in cider.

KEN That's right, Noel. I've always done it.

NOEL Some people might say it's a strange thing to do . . . What does your wife think of it?

KEN TAYLOR

KEN   She doesn't mind. I've been putting things in cider since we first met.

NOEL   Haaaaaaa. (These letters represent an exhalation from the lung which is not so much a laugh as a sharp blast of noisy moist air . . . the key to its success is that it stops very abruptly.)

NOEL   What was the first thing you put in cider?

KEN   Oh yes, now the very first thing I put in cider was a breadbin. Yes, that's right.

NOEL   Haaaaaaaaa . . . Now, Ken, if there was one thing that you would really like to put in cider what would that be?

KEN   Oh, that's easy . . . I'm a keen musician and I'd like to put my organ in cider.

NOEL   Haaaaaa . . . Ken Taylor!

Applause. Noel walks away from Ken's set back to the main set.

NOEL   Now every week we get hundreds of letters from people with hobbies or collections that involve animals or pets or simply nuts . . . Well, let me introduce you now to a gentleman whose collection very cleverly combines animals and nuts . . . Mr Chris Bell.

Noel arrives at Chris's set. This consists of a large white screen six foot square with the name 'Chris Bell' on it, a large school dining table and a school chair. On the table are 12 to 15 pottery horses, each of which is drawing (i.e. via a harness) a different type of nut, for example:

walnut	*cob*
peanut	*brazil*
doughnut	*coconut*
almond	*pecan*
cashew	*macadamia*
hazelnut	*Clive James nut*
chestnut	*wingnut*
tigernut	*monkeynut*
pistachio	*winegaurdnut*

NB *During the following piece Chris Bell is going to make a number of puns based on nuts and horses. These have been helpfully placed in quotation marks. Each time one is said a scorekeeper on the screen (i.e. like the one that keeps tag of the number of score draws when the football results are coming through on Saturday* Grandstand) *clicks over to record the pun. This scorekeeper reads 'Score Draws'. Also after each pun a reception bell rings to log the pun audibly.*

NOEL   So Chris, what exactly is it that you collect?

CHRIS   (Vic) (in the manner of an incredibly cocky youthful Max Bygraves and with a tendency to be overly intimate both vocally and visually) Noel, let me tell you. What I do is I collect horsedrawn nuts . . .

NOEL   That's amazing. Let's have a 'pecan' at them.

CHRIS   Yes, Noel, let me tell you, I'm 'nuts' about this little lot . . . I could talk till I'm 'horse' about them . . . Now, Noel, come here, you're a lovely little man . . . Now I got 'saddled' with this little lot when my Aunt 'Hazel' who lived in 'Brazil' died in the 'reign' of Louis-Philippe the 'pear'-shaped king.

At this point the score draw counter turns and the bell rings in acknowledgement of him saying 'pear'. At this exact point a pre-recording is run of Bruce Forsyth saying: 'You get nothing for a pair, not in this game.' (NB This Forsyth insert should be filmed when Bruce is doing his bit in Show 1 as part of the Victorian dream sequence.)

NOEL   That's fascinating . . . So what's this one – 'cashew'?

CHRIS   Bless, you, Noel . . . Yes it is, you lovely little man . . . You like looking at my nuts, don't you, Noel?

NOEL Haaaaaaa . . . Ladies and gentlemen, Chris Bell.

Applause, with camera remaining on Noel to follow him back to main set.

NOEL *(as he walks back to the main set)* And now, ladies and gentlemen, we've all been waiting for . . . Yes, it's time to present this week's wobbly melon award.

Applause as Noel mounts himself behind a podium which has a drawing of Noel Edmonds (provided by Vic) with the words 'Noel Edmonds' below and on the top has a nice water melon (8 inches high). This melon can be made to shake and vibrate upon Noel pulling a 14-inch lever that is situated on the side of the podium.

NOEL And tonight's wobbly melon award . . . *(activates melon wobbling facility)* goes to a man

nice pink draylon shirt

D.L.T.

High Style 'Trucker' Jeans

OR

A tight Blue 'Boiler' Suit.

who you'll all know as Clement Attlee . . . Ladies and gentlemen, please welcome Mr Clement Attlee . . .

Applause.

Enter Dave Lee Travis (Vic) (see drawing) carrying a framed picture of Noel Edmonds from his DJ years (i.e. with big shirt collars, etc). This picture is about 4 ft x 3 ft. One cannot see the picture quite yet.

NOEL Oh no, not you *(pathetically acting as if surprised)*.

DLT *(with his arm around Noel)* All right, me old chum?

NOEL Oh no, what are you up to?

DLT You thought you'd got one over on me *(turning round the painting)*.

NOEL What's that?

DLT It's an old picture of you, where you look slightly different.

NOEL Oh, no . . . take it away . . . Where did you get that from?

DLT Revenge is sweet. *(Continues to taunt Noel with the painting and chases him as Noel tries to get away. Suddenly three walking tomatoes enter the fray and begin dancing around Noel's feet.)*

Close-up of Noel.

NOEL Oh no, it's gone crazy. It's the tomatoeeze . . . See you next week.

DLT Yeah, bye.

DLT, Noel and the tomatoeeze continue to fool around interspersed with shots of the set, the wobbling melon, the horsedrawn nuts, etc., as the following credits roll . . .

Written by Mustard Gas

Script Associate Town Gas

Cameraman Mr Mix Up

Tilting provided by
Bongo Jim and his Peppery Penguin

Union Jacks supplied by
Grumpies Magic Vinegar Pot

Producer Crab with Bronze Hand

Director Arse Magic

A Terrys Chocolate Orange Production

At the end of the titles the BBC globe (circa 1969, blue and black with the word 'COLOUR' underneath) appears. BBC announcer voice-over . . .

VOICE-OVER   And now tonight's feature film, a war-time drama starring Michael Redgrave ner ner ner ner ner ner ner ner British airfield.

EYEBROW CURTAINS

Camera pulls back to show Vic and Bob viewing the TV from behind. Bob leans forward to turn off the TV as Vic turns to face the camera.

VIC   That was real mega cool TV that, Bob. Watcha think, Bob?

Bob turns to camera revealing that his eyebrows have grown downwards obscuring his vision by forming two eye curtains. (See drawing entitled 'eyebrow curtains'.)

BOB   Unfortunately, Vic, I missed it because my eyebrows suddenly grew, obscuring my view.

VIC   Yes, I can see that now.

Move to close-up of Bob's face with Vic's pointing hand moving deliberately from one eye to the other.

VIC   You have an eyebrow curtain here *(hand moves to other eye)* and here.

BOB   Yes, I understand now. And I'll leave with those two 16-year-old police officers . . . *(unseen)* there and there.

Bob gets up and leaves in a forthright manner but not as forthright, say, as a woman resigning from work following a manhandling incident in the stock room involving – yes, you've guessed it – Colin Mayhew from time and motion. What is it about him? I mean he's happily married to Jean who works in the canteen at the Flymo factory . . . mind you, she's no angel . . . Do you remember in 1978 (I think) she was had up for manhandling Mr Peanut when he came to the factory to give a lecture on oral hygiene? . . . But even then . . . I mean they've got two lovely kids, Nikki and Cliff (I think) . . . although having said that Cliff does have an oddly peanut-shaped head and an impeccable dental record . . . and Nikki is reputed to be having group sex with Professor Pelican and his mate Nutty Nandoo and his magic tandoori turban.

CUT TO

ADRIAN MARSH

Adrian (played by classically trained actor, James Moir) and his mate Amanda, in his electronically powered dustbin, are already in position on stage.

ADRIAN   Listen, right, I've got certain beliefs, right . . . Some of you may think certain of these beliefs are a bit strange . . . Like, you see, five million years ago we was all, like, sort of, like, gnomes . . . and we had a central eye, like, that could see through the walls of pyramids and glean secret information, right . . . Now these secrets have been lost . . . or – now this is a big or – or have they been stolen by the . . . C . . . I . . . D . . . ? We will never know the answer to this and many other . . . Oh . . . *(spotting Amanda Withington, played by alternative comedian Robert Mortimer in his dustbin beside him)* Hi, Amanda, man.

AMANDA   Hi, Adrian. Nice new theory, man.

ADRIAN   Wow, Mandy. That is some bucket, man.

AMANDA   It's a dustbin, man.

ADRIAN   Oh, wow maximus strangus, Amanda. Right, guys, what strange item have you brought today?

AMANDA   Here, check this out, Adrian. My lady give it me . . . I think it's strangely beautiful.

(Amanda hands to Adrian one of those white and pink knitted poodles that goes over an unsightly toilet scourer or bleach bottle to make people believe a small static poodle is living in the bathroom.)

ADRIAN   Wow, man . . . what is it?

AMANDA   I'm glad you like it. Listen, guys, what it is, right, is like a woollen poodle, right for covering your Harpic.

ADRIAN   Oh, maximus strangus, Doctor. I get it. So, like, guests would think there's a little poodle sitting on your cistern.

AMANDA   No, man, not on my sister – in the loooooooooo.

ADRIAN   Wow, what a cover-up. Man, where does your lady get such strange things from?

AMANDA   She works, right, like, for this toiletries company and she gets, like, freebies. She says to her boss guy, 'Here, have you got any freebies for me' and they arrive more or less directly.

ADRIAN   Oh, wow, freebies pronto. You got any other freebies in that bucket?

AMANDA   *(pulling out a big yellow sponge in the shape of a foot)* Well, she gets loads of these.

ADRIAN   Oh, man . . . largus footus . . . that is not a human foot.

AMANDA   No, Adrian, it's a novelty sponge freebie.

ADRIAN   Freebie maybe . . . but, if you will, imagine this Cinderella style scenario: 'Cinders, will this foot fit your leg?'

AMANDA   No, fair prince, for it is a novelty sponge.

ADRIAN   Of course it won't for it is too large to be from a human . . . It can only mean one thing, Amanda . . . that giants exist.

AMANDA   Adrian, it's a novelty sponge. They make thousands of them.

ADRIAN   Amanda, you are a goodus friendus, but you overlook one vital fact: where did they get the first mould for these now popular novelty bathtime . . . Think about that next time you are in the bath . . . Strange . . . Hold on, where's my hamburger? . . .

AMANDA   *(pulling burger from bin)* Here, have one of mine.

Adrian eats burger quietly for a short period.

ADRIAN   *(in Paul Whitehouse old get voice)* Here, Mand, have you got any money I can have?

AMANDA   What for?

ADRIAN   I want to go shopping.

AMANDA   No, Adrian.

Adrian returns to eating burger.

AMANDA   Adrian, do you want to get in the bucket?

ADRIAN   Yeah . . . *(Adrian gets in bucket.)*

CUT TO

BOB GIVES BIRTH

Bob is lying on the desk preparing to give birth. Vic is standing behind the desk enjoying a delicious dairy cream horn. Bob's lower half is covered by a green screen sheet.

VIC   Hello, sailors. I'm enjoying a delicious cream horn whilst Bob here is giving birth.

BOB   That's right. I hope it's not an ape like last time.

Enter small barrel-chested bespectacled middle-aged man (from the 1937 period) carrying a Gladstone bag and wearing a double-breasted pinstripe suit.

MAN   What's going on here? Eating a delicious cream horn whilst this man gives birth . . . I'll take over here. *(Man takes cream horn out of bag and stands next to Vic and commences eating it.)*

Enter second man dressed identically to first ONLY FATTER.

2ND MAN   Wilson, what are you doing here eating a delicious cream horn whilst this man gives birth potentially to an ape? I'll take over here. *(Again second man joins Vic and first man enjoying a cream horn behind the desk.)*

Enter third man dressed identically to the other two ONLY FATTER.

3RD MAN   Wilson Bradshaw, what are you doing eating cream horns whilst this man gives birth to what on first appearance may well be an ape. *(The third man joins Vic and the other two men behind desk eating delicious cream horns.)*

VIC   Bob, I've finished my cream horn so I'll go and do the interview. Will you be all right? . . .

BOB   Yes, of course, Vic.

(Vic glances under sheet.) I think it is an ape.

BOB   Never mind, you can't have enough of them.

Camera follows Vic over to interview area. This features:

a) *two of those office chairs where you operate a lever and they rise up and then you release the lever to allow the chair to slowly fall down to its original height.*
b) *a low coffee table.*

On the table is a silver cake-stand (which is quite valuable) and a white plate with a 9-inch stack of the largest popadoms that are available. On the cake-stand are a variety of cream cakes all of which, of course would be lovely with a nice cup of tea . . . except perhaps the meringue which is probably nicer with a glass of milk.

CELEBRITY GUEST: TOM SELLECK

VIC Ladies and gentlemen, please welcome my special guest Mr Tom Selleck.

Enter Bob wearing black gaffer tape moustache and eyebrows and a flattened afro-effect hairpiece (for he is playing the part of Tom the Selleck).

Tom and Vic greet each other and sit down. Interestingly it becomes clear that Tom speaks with a Lancashire accent similar to Fred Dibner (the steeplejack).

VIC Well, Tom, tell us about your new film *Revenge of the Running Killing Man*.

TOM Great question, Vic . . . It's about lumberjacks. Do you know what they are?

VIC No.

TOM Well they're woodcutters.

VIC Well, I've used cut wood.

TOM Well, you know what a woodcutter does then. What does he do?

VIC He cuts wood.

TOM That's right . . . you're a bright lad, Vic, you'll go far if you go for it . . . now watch . . . what's happening in the film now? *(Tom mimics shivering from being cold.)*

VIC You're very, very cold.

TOM That's right, Vic . . . So what did I do . . . I went for it . . . I chopped up some wood . . . I didn't want to, but it was cold so I went for it . . . Do you see what I'm getting at? . . . I went for it . . . Where do you get your chopped wood?

VIC From my local hardware store.

TOM You see I can't do that because . . . *(turns directly to camera, then utilizing a jaunty George Formby style voice)* I was stuck in a forest in the middle of nowhere.

VIC But, Tom, back to the film. Is it a thriller, a Hooray Henry film *(standing up and bending over fiddling with arse)*, Monty Python *(sitting down)* or just a straightforward Dr Who?

TOM I like that, you're going for it . . . but just going back a bit, like . . . You know I was talking about going for it . . . well, I've noticed that there's some of those cream cakes on the table, you know, naughty but nice . . . and you might have said, no I won't have one . . . it's naughty . . . but me I would just go for it . . . you know, it will be OK . . . just go for it . . . Anyway, Vic, carry on.

VIC I was just asking what sort of film it was.

TOM Another good question, Vic . . . you're going for it . . . But, here think on . . . You see, I woke up one morning and I were blind . . . and you know I was a bit like you, Vic . . . I ummed and ahhd about it . . . You know, got a bit bored with it . . . Then I said, no I'm going to go for it and I strode into that bloody doctor's and said sort these buggers out, Doc . . . the pair of them . . . and he did, you see . . . 'cos I went for it. Anyway, you were saying?

VIC Who directed the film? Was it Speilberg, some Hooray Henry *(standing up and fiddling with arsehole)*, Monty Python *(sitting down)* or just Dr Who?

TOM You've gone for it . . . I like it . . . I'll answer your question. I like you . . . You're a young man . . . partially good-looking . . . Have you thought of taking a wife? . . . You should go for it, you know . . . Hey, yes, it's like in the film . . . You mentioned the film earlier didn't you? . . . Well, look at me in the film *(mimics kissing a lass)* . . . You see, I'm kissing a beautiful Hollywood actress and that wouldn't have happened if I hadn't gone for it . . . Are you beginning to see?

VIC So who was the director?

TOM Good question . . . I'll tell you *(facing directly to the camera)*. It was Mmmmmmickey Rooney . . . I tell you another thing: Second World War . . . tiny little country like us took on the might of the Third Reich . . . no chance, they thought, but we went for it . . . I don't know if you've read the Bible, like, but there's some good stories in there about people going for it . . . You know, like Moses parting the Red Sea . . . No chance, the people thought, but he went for it . . . used his magic wand . . . Or the time he wanted to set fire to a bush . . . He didn't have any matches or a Zippo or 'owt . . . but he went for it . . . used his magic wand again . . .

As Tom rambles on Vic gets up and begins to walk back over to the scene of the potential primate birth. As he walks . . .

VIC Well, I've been talking to Tom Selleck about his new film *The Running Killing Man* directed by *(in Formby voice)* Mmmmickey Rooney.

Vic is now standing behind the desk. On the desk are a number of items Bob has given birth to (see song below).

VIC How did the birth go?

BOB Absolutely fine as usual. No complications.

VIC *(excitedly)* So what is it?

BOB Come here, Vic, let's take a look.

SONG: 'LET'S HAVE A LOOK AT IT'

I love the smell of an ape,
I love the smell of a grape,
I love the smell of a tapeworm,

So come on now, let's have a look at them,
Come along, Bob, these are your children,
Come along then let's see what else you have
     bore.

The boys walk away from the desk to where the remaining items are displayed in the manner that game show prizes might be.

I love the smell of a Ford Fiesta,
I love the smell of Frank Bough's wife Nester,
I love the smell of a horsedrawn necklace,

Come along, Vic, don't they look lovely?
Yes they do, Bob, what a lovely family,
but please, Vic, let's not have any more.

THE BRA MEN: 'FLAT 32B'

A postman is seen, from behind, at a front door which is no. 32 and has four bells marked A, B, C & D.

He is about to ring one of the bells when the door is opened by Pat.

POSTMAN Ah, hello. Are you 32B?

PAT *(wearing shirt and guardedly putting his hand over top two buttons and drawing the shirt in)* None of your business . . . what are you saying like? . . . That I'm flat . . . *(taking parcel from postman)* You can keep your parcel.

Pat shuts door in postman's face, taking a parcel inside with him.

SHOW

Dear Sirs,

There was a time when the rolling downs and fertile valleys of Kent were the home of an established and flourishing soft fruit industry. Blackcurrants and bilberries were exported by the tonne to the chateaux of the courtiers to Louis XIV. Cherries by the shipload, were sent by the shipload to the table of Mahatma Gandhi the Margerarhji of India to flavour his curry. Gooseberries, picked gingerly from their poisonous thorned stems by peasants wearing clay hats, were transported by the vanload to tart up the salad stop at the great herring disaster viewing booth on board the *Queen Mary*. Loganberries and raspberries pressed, pulped and pummelled by peasants wearing pewter caps were used to dye the ceremonial gowns of the royal giants.

Yes, this was the flourishing soft fruit industry (SOFRU) and we all thought it would never end.

It was, however, always labour intensive. The peasants moved away and found employment in the exciting new world of soft deer. Yes, the roe deer, the fallow deer, the Muntjak, all so easily crushed and transformed into a wonderful steaming purée. The Body Shop couldn't get enough, nor could the public and soon other soft mammals were being sought out and slaughtered.

But who am I to be processing this information? I'll tell you who . . .

. . . I'm the bloke who pummelled the otter with a spade at the end of Ring of Bright Water . . . All right . . . so don't start telling me I know nowt about the demise of the soft fruit industry . . . I do . . . So you little Hitlers can take your Magic Markers and your little half-eaten packets of dog muck and Sellotape it to the funnel of Woody Woodpecker's U-boat.

Yours faithfully,

Captain Bonkers
Lieutenant Loobrush
Sergeant Shoehorn
King Ketchup
Mr Potty

PS Salted crisps . . . in this weather!
PPS Wot no Vymura . . . shame on you.

OPENING TITLES

VOICE-OVER   Ladies and gentlemen, who knows where my rosemary grows? If anyone does it's these two . . . Please welcome the inventors of the horse-drawn leg warmer . . . It's Reeves and Mortimer!

Music strikes up and comedians enter stage singing the following song:

NB *As they sing they illustrate the song by pointing to a re-creation on the stage of a small boy who has fallen down the side of a cliff and lies unconscious on a ledge and a separate scene of the boy's mother at the top of the cliff asleep on a tartan rug.*

The woman is wearing a magician's assistant's glittery one-piece swimming costume type outfit (red) with fishnet tights, red high heels and red gloves. Appropriate hairstyle and make-up are equally apparent. It is clear that she has been drinking heavily as in her hand is a bottle of Gordon's gin and beside her a pile of various spirit bottles.

The boy is dressed in a blue child's glittery Elvis Presley catsuit and sunglasses.

SONG: 'EMERGENCY MOUNTAIN RESCUE' (PART ONE)

Chorus (in a real heavy rock style)

Don't slip on loose muesli
Don't drink and sleep on the scree
Keep clear of clergy on a cliff-top
Don't let your children run free

Verse (spoken above finger-clicking groove):

VIC   This is a story 'bout a beautiful little lady called Carol Ann.

BOB That's right. Now Carol Ann was doing OK and she topped up her benefit money, with the odd show as a magician's assistant.

VIC Yeah, but that work dried up all of a sudden when the Amazing Mr Potty was sent to prison. Understandably she turned to gin.

BOB *(walking over to find the sleeping woman)* And so in a drunken stupor and as if to review her life she took her young child Johnny to a cliff-top overlooking the Vale of Pickering . . . For a while they enjoyed the view together but soon her sight became blurred and Carol Ann fell asleep clutching a bottle of gin to her breast.

VIC *(still centre stage)* That's right, but where was Johnny? Let me tell you. Earlier that day a young clergyman had come to that very same spot to enjoy his breakfast but suddenly recalling a particularly exciting sermon delivered by Sir Harry Secombe the previous day his arm jerked involuntarily and loose muesli was spilt on to the ground. *(Close-up of Vic's finger pointing to some loose muesli on the makeshift cliff-top.)*

BOB Johnny approached the cliff edge cautiously.

VIC But the soles of his little brothel creepers were too thick to sense the loose muesli beneath his feet.

BOB His grip was lost, he began to fall.

VIC The wind caught his little Elvis Presley costume and sent him crashing on to a blimmin' ledge. *(We see the little boy unconscious on the ledge.)*

BOB He didn't have time to cry out but, I tell you, ladies and gentlemen, if he had . . . this is what he would have said:

Don't slip on loose muesli
Don't drink and sleep on the scree
Keep clear of clergy on the cliff-top
Don't let your children run free

Carol Ann kept on boozing
Didn't hear a word we said
Got drunk on a cliff-top
Now little Elvis is dead

Don't blame the clergyman
For leaving muesli on a mountain
The blame lies with Carol Ann
She just lay back boozing

Yeah.

VIC & BOB

Vic Reeves and Bob Mortimer then travel fleet-footedly to the desk. They welcome the audience and proceed to tell the following funny gags:

VIC *(holding up a piece of correspondence)* Bob, have you seen this letter?

BOB No.

VIC Look *(pointing to an individual letter)*, there, it's a 'G'.

BOB Oh, Vic, that is so funny. Interesting, I got a letter this morning . . . nothing special . . . just a couple of lines. *(Holds up letter to audience revealing that there are just two thick black lines drawn on it – 3 mm wide, 13.5 cm long, 4.2 cm apart and positioned horizontally with their axis central to a piece of blank A4 paper.)*

Extreme close-up of Vic and Bob alternately laughing manically as in Shows 1 *and 2. After five seconds of this close-up laughter cut to wider shot of audience looking bored stiff. (This audience should maybe not be our own audience but perhaps an audience aged between 28 and 51 years without any trendy youngsters or pensioners.) Cover with dubbed audience laughter.*

After three seconds of audience cut dubbed laughter and cut to a further two seconds of Vic and Bob laughing. Making a total of ten seconds in all. This isn't a great deal of time. A close friend might be quite hurt if you only spent ten seconds waving him goodbye as he left to face a court martial in Gibraltar. Having said that if one was to scratch one's arsehole for ten seconds at, say, a wedding (especially if you were the vicar), in Parliament (especially if you were the PM during Question Time) or at a cup final (especially if you were the penalty taker), well, ten seconds would seem like an aeon.

VIC Oh, Bob, that's very funny indeed. Hey, Bob, don't let me forget to check the flights before we go.

BOB Why? Are we flying home tonight?

VIC No, I'm playing darts.

At this point Brian May ex Queen axe-man but now pursuing a successful solo career as a police cork whilst continuing his stormy relationship with ex-Navy Lark and survivor of the great herring disaster Anita Dobson, pops up from behind the desk with shampoo in his hair. He has the words 'Brian May' written on his forehead. His hair is covered in foaming shampoo.

For a period of five seconds the comedians wash his hair and laugh. Cut to three seconds of audience with canned laughter as above. Cut to two seconds of hairwashing. Brian May disappears unfussily. Again a total period of ten seconds will have elapsed. As we mentioned earlier this isn't a great deal of time, though when you think about it, a close friend might be quite hurt if you only let him play with your Matchbox Motorized Motorway for just ten seconds. Having said that, if one was to find oneself suddenly and inexplicably nude at, say, a book signing (especially if you were first in the queue), a courtroom (especially if you were an alibi witness in an indecent exposure case), a school speech day especially if you were the headmaster and had three, yes three, arses – just imagine the pupils delight as they chant:

Sir has three, yes three, arses; Sir has three, yes three, arses)

BOB That is such a funny one, Vic.

VIC (with cigarette in hand) Bob, have you got a light, please?

BOB No, but just throw that away and you'll be a cigarette lighter.

Vic immediately commences grating a 1lb block of that cheese that is, like, part orange and part yellowy white (that type of yellowy white that comes out of a fly when it dies following impact e.g. from windscreen, book or chopsticks if you happen to be that karate kid) into a nice size 12 brown leather brogue.

At the same moment Bob turns on a food processor liquidizing unit (a loud one).

After 4 seconds of grating and 2.5 seconds of liquidization cut to our bored audience who are now 50 per cent less (i.e. to give impression that half have left). After 2.83 seconds cut back to the comedians who finish their grating and blending.

VIC Bob . . . Er, um, that was terrible . . . But it was slightly saved by the fact that it was fortunately only 10 seconds long.

At this point Vic and Bob repeat their observations noted above on the debate as to whether ten seconds is a long period of time or a short period of time. This will end with our boys singing the schoolboy chant, 'Sir has got three bottoms'.

THE BRA MEN: 'THE TRAFFIC WARDEN'

Pat and Dave are going on holiday in their Triumph Dolomite with their luggage on a roof rack.

A female traffic warden (Ioni) is beside a brown Triumph, preparing to attach a parking ticket to it. On top of the car are some suitcases which are very badly strapped to a roof rack.

Enter Dave carrying another suitcase. He ignores warden and begins to place the suitcase on car roof.

DAVE   *(noticing traffic warden)* Oh, come on, love . . . I'm just away on me holidays.

WARDEN   *(with sympathetic look)* Oh, all right then . . . could I just ask is that an old Triumph?

DAVE   Why, it's quite a new one if it's any of your business. *(clutching shirt as per usual)* Have you got a problem with me bra or something?

WARDEN   I'm sorry, we're talking at cross purposes. *(Laughs.)*

DAVE   Oh, something funny, is there? Just 'cos me bra's a bit old-fashioned.

WARDEN   There's no need to get nasty.

By this time Pat is next to car fiddling with the straps.

WARDEN   *(pointing towards Pat)* And you make sure you tighten those straps before you leave.

PAT   What are you saying like? . . . I'm wearing a strapless for me holidays . . . *(approaches warden)* There's no straps to tighten . . . You're just looking for trouble when there is none . . . *(grabbing parking ticket)* . . . you can keep your ticket . . .

WARDEN   Suit yourself. *(Turns and walks off.)*

CUT TO   Vic and Bob still at desk (not like 'static' at desk but, as it were, 'have remained' at desk).

BRIAN MAY

VIC   Mmm, so straight away, no delay, what was the timing, Brian May?

Brian May is now sat about 10 feet from desk on a seat that allows him to kneel so that he can have a special pair of Guy Fawkes dummy legs attached.

BRIAN   One minute, twenty-nine point six four seconds, Sir. *(For he speaks in the manner of an army sergeant major.)*

CUT   Back to desk.

BOB   Aren't there a lot of magazines on the shelves these days, Vic?

VIC   Wooooooaaaaaaaagfggghh, yes there are, Bob . . . *(back to normal voice)* and we've been reviewing two of this week's new publications, haven't we, Bob?

BOB   Wooooooooaaaaaaaagfggghh, we have Vic . . . Yes, two welcome additions to the hairstyling genre of glossies . . . *Centreparting Monthly.*

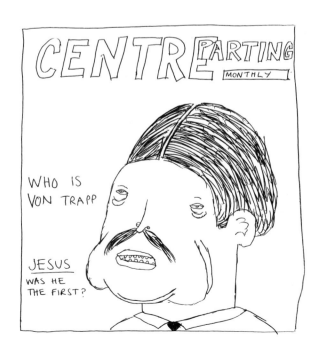

VIC And *Sideparting Weekly*.

BOB Right . . . *Centreparting Monthly* as you would guess is dedicated to the world of centrally parted hairs. At £2.50 it's not cheap but the advert to article ratio was very good. The editorial was clear and concise and some of the aerial photography was simply stunning, Vic.

VIC At £1.60 *Sideparting Weekly* represents good value. Again, adverts have been kept to a minimum and the articles, although sometimes rather difficult to understand, were generally of a high standard. The panoramic photography was absolutely breathtaking. An innovation I particularly enjoyed was that page 30 had been cut into the shape of a Webley automatic pistol.

BOB That's a good idea . . . Mind you, page 17 of *Centreparting* is actually printed on a thick ginger beard.

VIC Really innnovative, Bob . . . I've noticed page 17 of my magazine has lettering made out of cockroach antlers.

BOB Wow, I like that one . . . Having said that, my page 52 is fitted with a transparent motorized

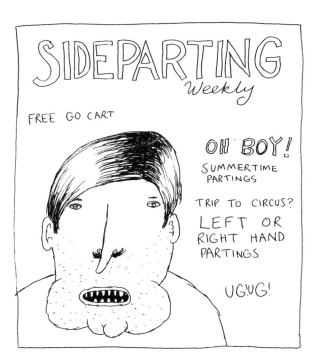

fish cake which runs across the page magnifying each word as you read . . . That's got to be good news for the partially sighted centreparter.

VIC *(taking the challenge)* Page 178 of my publication is fitted with an electronic, motorized, talking, fluorescent, weeping clam that, when you remove its belt, dances gracefully across the page pointing out the most salient points . . . That's got to be a boon for the sideparter in a hurry.

BOB So, Vic, two new publications. Which would you recommend?

VIC It's got to be my *Sideparting Weekly*.

BOB So you're poo-pooing my parting publication, are you?

VIC Bit of a swizz, lacks snazz, lacks pazzaz, got to poo pah.

BOB You're being pernickety, pal. You poo pah my periodical when yours is pompous prittle prattle.

VIC Piffle you, podgy pansy . . . It's not pompous prittle prattle.

At this point Uncle Peter suddenly emerges accompanied by his girlfriend. Peter is sporting an elaborate heavily bouffant Quentin Crisp/ Algernon Swinburne type hairstyle. He is wearing a bottom-rib length, slightly crumpled home-made green felt cape and white polo neck. He is flamboyantly and pontificariously acting in a high-falutin manner by extravagantly using a Vicks nasal stick.

PETER Poo poo all of them . . . *(indicating with hand his hairstyle)* You can't learn style from a book . . . You've either got it or you haven't . . . Isn't that right, love? . . . Move on to the next item.

BOB Peter, stop it. You know what happened last time you got fancy notions.

VIC Yes, that's when they found that drunken bluebird in your vice.

PETER No, no, please don't send me back to the dark place . . . *(turning to leave)* Come on, love, ignore them . . . *(as leaving)* My very, very, very dear friend Mel Gibson is waiting in reception.

BOB And we'll be giving away one month's free subscription to the viewer who can answer this question correctly. Centrepartings are:

a Just a bit of fun
b A wind up
c Eerie
d Central

At this point Vic has sneaked off to replace the actor playing Brian May. He interrupts Bob as follows:

BRIAN Excuse me . . . Could you help me? . . . Could you come to me?

Bob joins Brian at his throne.

BOB What's the matter, Brian?

BRIAN I'm sorry, I can't get off on me own.

BOB Why's that?

BRIAN I've got Guy Fawkes leg.

BOB Oh you have, haven't you . . . How long have you had it?

BRIAN Look, please, I'd rather not discuss it here in front of all these people . . . I used to be a killer queen, you know . . . Is there not somewhere private we can go?

BOB Hey, Bri, I know it's hard for you but if you could just hold on I know two people who just might be able to help.

BRIAN Oh, really? Whose that?

BOB Otis Redding and Marvin Gaye.

Otis and Marvin appear on monitor.

OTIS AND MARVIN

OTIS All right, Bob, yes, we're sat here again watching them ships come in and then go out again . . . We haven't seen one come in today yet but we haven't given up hope, have we, Marvin?

MARVIN To tell you the truth, Otis, I couldn't care less . . . I've been sat here five weeks now watching ships come in, stop, and then go out again . . . I'm bored stiff.

OTIS Oh, Marvin, how could you . . . You said you were having a lovely time watching the ships.

MARVIN Oh, I know, but couldn't we just once do what I want to do. Maybe go down the Grapevine and listen to people spreading rumours?

OTIS Marvin, really that's a terrible place. That Smokey Robinson hangs out there and I don't want you hanging around with his type . . . You know what happened last time . . . Now look out for ships coming in and then going out again.

MARVIN Bollocks to you.

OTIS What?

MARVIN Nothing, I just thought I saw a ship coming in or was it going out?

OTIS Now then, lads . . . Oh, it's just you, Bob. Where's Vic?

BOB He's here pretending to be Brian May.

OTIS Oh all right, Vic, sorry, Brian . . . How can we help?

BOB Well, as you can probably see Brian here is suffering from Guy Fawking of this leg . . . and this leg.

OTIS Oh, right. That's a nasty case . . . Now, Brian, there are two types of leg Fawking, the most common one is caused by liquid build-up beneath the leg skin. Now the liquids could be the yoghurts, cooking oils, any of the drinks family, for example 'it's frothy, man' . . .

MARVIN   The other type of Fawking is caused by hardening of the leg due to the build-up of solids such as grit, woodchippings, hairbells, tools used in erotic woodcarvings, the brass fighting bear at the Grapevine . . .

OTIS   (interrupting) Yes, all right, Marvin, I think we get the idea . . . Now with both types of Fawking the leg is subject to swelling causing an effect often called sandbagging where the leg skin forms into a beautiful creaseless arch.

BOB   (examining the creaseless arch of the trouser) Wow, yes, Otis, it's perfectly creaseless, man.

OTIS   Now, Bob, have you got a pen?

BOB   Yes.

OTIS   Now we need to find out if it's solid or liquid Fawking.

BOB   OK. (He thrusts pen into leg and out spurts liquid which with a bit of luck and forward planning can be operated by Vic from beneath the leg via the gift of Fairy Liquid and its ability to leave its bottle neatly and quickly at considerable speed.)

OTIS   Ahhh, it's liquid-based.

MARVIN   Yes and that would tie in because liquid leg is usually caused by standing still for long periods.

OTIS   Correct, Marvin, and I'm afraid to say that Brian was always the idle git in the group Queen.

BOB   Is there any cure?

OTIS   The only cure is leg exercise . . . and what better music to exercise to than the sweet Welsh voice of Bonnie Tyler. (Cue music 'I Need a Hero (Till the Morning Light)' by Bonnie Tyler.)

Bob commences to exercise Brian's legs. In doing so he will place them in some hilariously awkward and precarious positions. But Brian and Bob are happy. There should be three cameras on the duo changing along with the song. As camera angle changes the duo try to follow to the best of their abilities with hilarious results.

The duo continue to do this for an appropriate period of time, i.e. until the hilarity begins to turn, firstly, to a mild irritation then simple annoyance and then, finally, violent involuntary vomiting and nausea (you know that terrible feeling of edginess brought on by qualms).

As soon as the qualm period arrives Brian gets up from behind the chair and commences a comical dance utilizing hand-held versions of the Guy Fawked legs in front of a waist-high white screen.

During the final moments of this dance Brian and Bob let out a couple of rousing primal screams each which could cause nausea if anyone has any qualms about them. (The actual screams themselves may be best put on in post-production.)

As Bry and Bob receive their applause at the end of this brief musical highlight we cut to:

SLADE IN RESIDENCE

Noddy, Don and Jimmy are in the lounge. Jimmy appears to be looking out of the window, Don is sticking a model truck together with glue at the table and Noddy is sitting on the sofa reading a paper.

NODDY   'Ere everybody listen to this. Available now from Reeves and Mortimer, it's a company right. Quack, Quack the Homebrew Duck. Delicious home brew lager in just seven seconds, that's bloody quick innit? And a sinkful of lager style drink in just seven seconds. It's unbelievable. How does that work then?

DON   I don't know, but it does.

NODDY   How do you know?

DON   I've got one that's how.

NODDY   You kept that quiet.

DON   Yeah, well do you blame me with you around? A sinkful wouldn't last two minutes.

NODDY   All right, if you've got one go and get it.

Don discovers that his hands are stuck to the table.

DON   I can't, Noddy, me hands stuck to the table with monster truck glue.

NODDY   Don't start with your practical jokes. If you've got a lager duck go and get it and let's have a look at it.

DON   I'm not kidding, Noddy, it's superglue.

NODDY   'Ere, Jimmy has he got one of them lager ducks

Jimmy makes a noise – we discover that he is not looking out of the window but his hands and face are stuck to the pane of glass. And he can only talk out of the side of his mouth.

DON   What are you staring at anyway you've been looking out of the window for the past four hours.

JIMMY   I'm not staring out of the window me face is stuck to the bloomin' window with Don's bloomin' monster truck bloomin' superglue.

NODDY   Oh don't you start as well. Come on let's have a look at you.

Noddy goes to get up out of his armchair and walks towards Jimmy.

NODDY   Ooh, I feels so strange I do. I feel like I'm carrying a sack of coal or something – it's so strange.

Noddy's trousers are stuck to the chair and eventually he gets pulled back as if attached to the chair by elastic.

NODDY   AAAAAAHHHH!

Noddy falls back into the chair and the chair tips over with him still attached to it. Dave enters carrying a tray of drinks.

DAVE   That's it come and get your Cup-A-Soups. Have you been farting again, Noddy? Honestly, don't. What have you done to my beautiful table. Get that cleaned up straight away. And you stop acting like a giddy goat will you? Noddy get off the comfy chair.

NODDY   I can't. Don's covered everything in monster truck glue.

DAVE   I'll stick you, Noddy.

Dave goes to move and finds his platforms stuck to the carpet. He sways around on them.

DAVE   Help! Noddy!

NODDY   Dave, I'm coming!

Noddy stands up with the armchair stuck to his arse. Overbalances and crashes forward against the shelving unit, head first.

DAVE   Oh no, me ceramic Harlequin. Jim, help us.

JIMMY   I'm coming, Dave.

Jimmy, hands and face still stuck to the glass levers the pane of glass out of its frame, swings round into the centre of the room and starts to walk forward – stepping on to the coffee table.

DAVE   Quickly. Oh no, not me coffee table.

JIMMY   Don't worry, mate.

DON   Don't worry, Dave, I'm coming

Don, hands still stuck to the table lifts it up over his head, staggers backwards, crashes against a different shelving unit. It crashes to the floor and Don falls forward breaking the table in two.

DAVE   What're you doing? Oh me pottery shire horse, anything but that.

The whole room has now been completely destroyed.

JIMMY   Hey, hang on a minute lads that glue wasn't sticky after all it was just one of Don's jokes.

DAVE   What!

NODDY   He's right, it's not even vaguely sticky.

DAVE   Look at that. I tell you what you really had us going then, Don.

DON   I did didn't I? I really had you going then didn't I? Didn't I, Noddy?

NODDY   You did, Don, it was a goodun!

DAVE   All right now we've had a laugh, right? Let's clear some space now and get some Cup-A-Soups down our necks.

ALL   Get down and get with it.

GREG AND CORKY (GREG ENDS UP IN COURT)

JUDGE   Case of Greg Mitchell, charged with aggravated robbery and a right load of old stress and grief. First prosecution witness, please.

Up pops Corky.

CORKY   All right, Judge, those fags all right?

JUDGE   Lovely smoke, thanks, Corky. So who planned the robbery?

CORKY   That poncy git Mitchell.

JUDGE   Can you see him in court?

CORKY   Yeah, there he is, you blind basket.

JUDGE   Hoi, less of your lip, Corky.

CORKY   Sorry, your honour, I was out of order.

JUDGE   Who got the money then?

CORKY   He did.

JUDGE   Thanks, Corky, I've heard enough. Gregory Mitchell, have you got anything to say?

GREG   It wasn't me.

JUDGE   Oh, shut it, you whinging toe rag. I hereby sentence you to be banged up for twenty years.

GREG   Twenty years . . . my wife's going to kill me.

CUT TO   Vic and Bob entering stage bringing with them the Reeves and Mortimer product display board. Vic quickly needles away from the board leaving Bob to manoeuvre it into its final position.

REEVES AND MORTIMER PRODUCTS

VIC   Well now, ladies and gentlemen, it's time to update you on some of the new products now available from the Reeves and Mortimer range.

BOB   That's right, Vic, and I'm very proud to announce that after months of waiting we can finally reveal tonight *(turns over page of display board)* the Reeves and Mortimer Shepherd's Crook Storage Cup. *(See drawing.)* On arriving

home from work simply plop your crook into the cup thus leaving both hands free to greet your wife and family in the proper manner.

VIC   Not only that, Bob, but a mild acid in the bottom of the cup will rinse away all unwanted dog dirt from the staff tip and deposit it on this nearby tortoise.

BOB   But what if the tortoise moves, Vic?

VIC   It won't, Bob . . . believe me.

VIC   Bob, you're a keen cook and you keep finches . . .

BOB   Yes.

VIC   Picture this horror scenario . . . You're slaving away over a hot steaming pot of stew . . . suddenly one of your baby finches drops into the pot. What do you do?

BOB   That's easy. I simply plunge my hand into

the boiling broth . . . Ahhh, that is a horror scenario.

VIC   Why?

BOB   *(turning to camera)* Why, I'll tell you why: dreadful hand scalding.

VIC   That's right, but now there is an alternative course of action in the form of *(turning page of display board)* the Reeves and Mortimer Stewscope. This high-powered kitchen endoscope can be plunged straight into the heart of any boiling stew to give you an 'as it happens' view of your dinner. In the case of your horror scenario, Bob, enabling you to assess whether the finch is alive or has passed away and can therefore be safely left in the pot to stew.

BOB   Great news for finch rearers . . . but that's only part of the story . . . If we look more closely at the 'what you see' view . . . There's that comb I lost last week, and my lighter and, yes, the tip of

CONVEX BOUNDARY FENCE
TAX EVASION SYSTEM

my winkle picker. If it hadn't been for the stewscope I'd never have been able to rock and roll again.

BOB   And finally, an exciting new product that is presently undergoing final testing but should be in your shops in the time for the harvest festival: the Reeves and Mortimer Convex Boundary Fence Tax Evasion System.

VIC   Imagine I'm a farmer nervously awaiting a visit from the taxman . . . Bob, you play the part of the taxman.

BOB   OK . . . Hello, Farmer, I've come to collect the tax on your large horses.

VIC   Oh, Taxman, there must be some mistake. Look through my new Reeves and Mortimer boundary fence and you will see that all my horses are tiny.

BOB   Yes, nothing but tiny horses and of course tiny horses are not a taxable item . . . I will leave

you in peace to enjoy your tiny livestock tax haven. *(Performs a very exaggerated wink to camera.)*

VIC   All the products on display will be available in good time for Lent.

Applause

At this point Vic spots what appears to be a lady's breast poking out from the side of the products presentation board. He tries to point this out to Bob by making the relevant hand to breast 'cup' and 'curve' motion (sufficient so audience are clear that it is a breast under scrutiny). Eventually Bob clocks it too. They want very much to touch it but due to heaps of common decency and an element of schoolboy nervosity they find it a very difficult thing to do . . . They discuss what they should do . . .

BOB   It is one, isn't it?

VIC   Yes, I believe it is . . . Have you ever seen one before?

BOB   Yes.

VIC   Oh, me too.

BOB   It's a nice one, isn't it?

VIC   Is it? . . . Oh, yes, it is.

Both rush back to the breast and have a close visual inspection.

BOB   Let's flush her out.

VIC   Oh, it's a woman, is it? Go on then.

Bob takes a carrot from his pocket and attempts to entice the woman out by dangling his carrot to the side of the breast as one might if one were trying to entice a horse out of one's new van. It doesn't work.

Vic takes over using a feather to tickle the breast whilst saying 'YOO HOO'. As he does this, Bob creeps round the front of the board in the style of *Nosferatu. Whatever it is he sees behind there it causes him pull the board away and make a bizarre facial expression.*

This leaves Vic in a crouched position tickling what is now revealed to be Uncle Peter's bare elbow. Peter is fast asleep with his arm resting on a broom.

We assure you that a male elbow presented in this manner is identical in every respect to Carly Simon's right breast circa 1963.

Vic kicks away the broom thus waking Uncle Peter.

UNCLE PETER   Eh? Who is Billy Smart? . . . Get off me land . . .

VIC   Peter, that's it. This time you've gone too far. Not only have you made me look stupid in front of an albeit small number of people but you've also caused a bogus arousal situation *(rotating Wilson style hand movement)* within me, but . . . hold on. Who is Billy Smart?

By this point Bob has joined Vic and Peter. It is clear from his expression that the Billy Smart legend is etched deeply on to his heart.

NB *During the following dialogue every time the name Billy Smart is said Uncle Peter ejaculates the utterance 'Eh?'*

BOB   Oh, Vic, Billy Smart . . . the greatest circus owner there ever was. You must remember the posters . . . Billy Smart's Circus coming to your town soon.

VIC   Billy Smart Whoooo?

PETER   Eh?

BOB   *(dreamily reminiscing)* Yes, Billy Smart . . . the big top . . . the ringmaster, the trapeze artist swinging neath the canvas . . .

At this point Vic, Bob and Peter are joined by the three 'doctors' who assisted Bob with his

childbirth at the end of Show 4 and another small Don Estelle type character. They don't all come on at once, however . . . Read on and see just 'how it works'. As each of these new men enter, the by now closely huddled group, the members of the group all turn awkwardly, interestedly and sharply to hear what the new man has to say.

1ST MAN   I couldn't help hearing you mention Billy Smart and his marvellous circuses. I always loved the lion tamer.

VIC   A what tamer? Who is this Billy Smart?

UNCLE PETER   Eh?

2ND MAN   How about the acrobats?

3RD MAN   Or my favourite, the human cannonball.

VIC   The human what? Look, who is he?

BOB   Billy Smart.

PETER   Eh?

BOB   You must remember . . . You know the tarts standing on horses' backs.

2ND MAN   Clowns in cars with square wheels.

VIC   *(falling quickly into mental disturbance)* What?

1ST MAN   Elephants walking in circles.

From this point onwards camera concentrates on Vic and his increasingly apparent fall into circus-induced nausea and qualms.

3RD MAN   And sometimes kneeling.

BOB   Seals seated on bar stools, catching balls.

2ND MAN   And the joy-filled faces of the innocent children as they gaze in wonder at the spectacle before them.

VIC   *(holding head with hands and clearly circus crazed)* Oh, no, there's children involved.

Close-up of Vic making a bit of a fuss . . . his eyes whirl . . . his legs turn to jelly and buckle . . . his head does the movement of a spinning top or perhaps spinning coin just before it runs out of its desire to spin . . . We see the view from Vic's eyes, which is the room spinning and lights flashing, as he collapses to the floor because, yes, we are entering a . . . dream sequence.

The important thing about this dream sequence is that it is filmed in the manner of a dream sequence in which The Prisoner (i.e. Patrick McGoohan) has been slipped a Mickey Finn by the Man From Uncle, you know the sort of thing, man . . . It's those so-called mind-bending crazy experiences such as a respectable middle-aged banker might have if he were fed mandrax and then attended a Yardbirds' concert at the UFO or Middle Earth clubs . . . you must know by now . . . Punch and Judy's coming very close to your face and laughing . . . fish-eye lens style visions . . . a dwarf waiter who takes the lid off his silver salver-revealing the head of Carlos Santana, then laughs in your face saying 'Jack and Jill went up the hill, ha ha ha ha' . . . A group of heavily made-up girls in denim bikini tops gather round to laugh at you . . . they are smoking elongated cigarettes and suddenly you realize that their faces are covered in . . . SPIDERS!

THE BILLY SMART'S CIRCUS DREAM SEQUENCE

The following images are seen in front of a screen of changing colour:

1. From bottom of frame up rears Billy Smart. He is wearing a white polo neck, has frightening ginger hair which is sprouting from his melon hat. He has utilized small vegetables to enhance his facial features (see drawing).

He rears up close to camera . . . retreats backwards and announces, 'I am Billy Smart and I welcome you to my broadbean circus.' His legs (false) rise up behind him and float about. His head goes back down leaving just his legs floating.

2. Into focus from behind the legs is revealed a man operating a wheel. He is wearing a light blue thick weave Acrylic V-neck jumper which is stretched over his hugely padded midriff. The wheel is being used as a 'Hobbybot' by his good friend Nude John Archer. A mystery item is on John's back. Sound effect is used to re-create the sound of an industrial circular saw cutting sheet steel for use when John's bottom comes into contact with the Hobbybot. When not in contact we hear the sound of a woodeny windmill mechanism.

Ken Taylor the Hobbybot operator is the same Ken Taylor from last week's Noel's Addicts. This week, however, he has much longer arms (no expensive effect required, please).

A pipe of smoke rises from the hobbybot when in contact with Nude John Archer's bottom.

We remain with this image for approximately 15 seconds.

3. A large head appears almost blocking entire view, and Ken and John are faded out of focus although their soundtrack might usefully be allowed to remain.

The large head is in fact the comedian Vic Reeves. His shoulders are nude. He has chocolate around his lips. He is wearing a subtle amount of blue eyeshadow. His hair is greased and combed forward. He is seen through the lens known as the fish-eye. He says the following:

VIC   Hello, ladies (exaggerated deep distorted wink). Any room for a little one?

Vic then drops down off bottom of screen and in

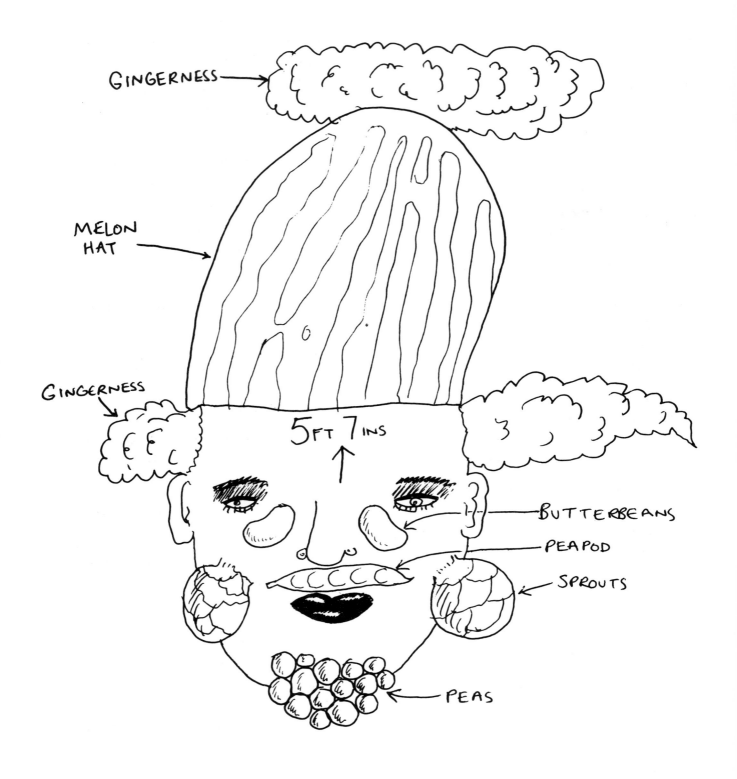

GINGERNESS

MELON HAT

GINGERNESS

5FT 7INS

BUTTERBEANS

PEAPOD

SPROUTS

PEAS

BILLY 'SMART'

the background, the following scene is brought into focus.

4. Between four and five men are standing in a close huddled group. One of them is Vic the other three or four are extras who are over 60. The three extras will wear whatever they turn up in and in no way must anyone attempt to influence them in their choice of garments for the day. Vic is wearing a grey raincoat, and shirt and tie, spectacles, small moustache and nicely combed hair.

Intermittently a Parisian trucell (about size 6 and preferably with ever so slightly lulled sleeve gambits) attached to transparent wire hovers above them and swoops in much the same way that the birds in the Hitchcock film The Birds used to enjoy doing.

The three extras shake their fists at it and try pathetically to grab it whilst making veiled drunken threats by use of various guttural noises and outbursts (no words). Vic does this as well.

In front of these men is Bob. He is bald . . . well not quite as we will draw a bit of hair on to the bald cap. He is naked but we can only see him from the waist up as the rest of his body is beneath floor level. In front of him is a white Victorian wash bowl with lovely warmy, mummy, sudsy water in it. Bob is gently splashing water on to his breasts, whilst saying in a vaguely Max Wall voice with a hint of recent breavement:

BOB   Oh Mummy, Oh Mummy dearest
          Oh Mummy, oh lovely Mummy

The above is in view for a 15-second period.

5. Billy Smart groiles into picture from side of screen with his face horizontal across the screen. Image three vanishes from view.

There are four Picnic bars revolving round his face giving the impression of either the four apostles searching for an English Tourist Board

approved vantage point in Hardy country or four pints of lager please, Philip, oh and have you got any of those new nuts that come in a hammock?

BILLY   Now, ladies and gentlemen, I present for yooooouuuu a nude picture of Mr Vic Reeves superimposed over an episode of The Sullivans.

Immediately cut to a still from The Sullivans with a picture of Vic's head on a nude woman's body superimposed on to it . . . for . . . hold on . . .

ONE FRAME ONLY
ONE FRAME ONLY
ONE FRAME ONLY

CUT TO   Vic makes his way to the desk and joins Bob reading the newspapers.

BOB   Who's Billy Smart?

VIC   He's the bloke who starred in me nightmare . . . I've just told you.

BOB   Oh, right. (Bob approaches Vic and gets very near his face and politely asks him) Now would you care for another sherry?

VIC   (poncily pondering the query) Hmm hm hm hm. . . . Yes, that would be nice.

As Bob goes to fridge to obtain more sherry two newspapers arrive through the door. Vic picks them up and as he does so his face comes into contact with the door. Unfortunately the door is very sticky and as he pulls his face away the area of door in direct contact with his face queels away with his face and then snaps back to its original position. This is achieved by having some double-sided tape in the appropriate position on a part of the door made from latex.

CUT TO   Bob where a similar latex queeling is occurring on the fridge door or a cupboard door. Vic and Bob are sat down on either end of the sofa reading the newspapers. They comment on the following features and headlines in the paper:

The price of the paper is 25p;
the date of the paper;
it is printed in Manchester;
one paper is heavier than the other.

CAT DIPS HEAD SLIGHTLY TO AVOID LOW HOOK

Dialogue here is improvised, you know, like *Whose Line Is It Anyway?* or the *Brain Drain* or *S&M* or *Boon* but will revolve around the following catarells.

Vic reads this headline and then farts . . . no fuss is made . . . he is after all in his own home . . . In Bob's paper a headline reads 'Naughty Cat Steals Doctor's Fish Supper'. They discuss these two headlines in some detail. Bob thinks it must have been stolen off a kitchen window ledge. Vic points out that it is naughty boys who steal off window ledges and then it's always meat pies not fish. Vic wonders if it's the same cat. Bob points out that there is nothing naughty about ducking under a low hook. Vic points out that the hook may have belonged to the surgeon or alternatively that the cat was hanging its head in shame due to guilt over the fish theft.

Bob thinks it unusual that any hook could be low enough to require a cat to dip its head. Cats, after all are quite low creatures. Vic points out that a) the wild cats such as lion and cheetah are quite high . . . thus the name big cats and b) if, for example, a crane driver had left his comb in his handbag on the ground he'd probably use his crane hook to try and hoist up the bag. Bob feels that the crane driver wouldn't do this as he would be wearing a safety hat. Vic realizes his error.

Bob wonders if perhaps the low hook belonged to a vehicle breakdown van and the cat was pretending to supervise the hooking of the hook on to the tow bar to impress his girlfriend . . .

You know, down a bit, left, oops, had to duck to avoid the hook scraping my head skin. Vic likes this explanation and excitedly points out that unwarranted hook supervision would only be attempted by quite a naughty cat, so perhaps it is the same cat in both stories.

The boyish men fall silent content with their deductions and then . . .

CUT TO   A man is seen from behind painting an oil painting on an easel. He is wearing a light brown linen suit and is holding a palette.

Camera closes in on him. He turns round revealing that he is ugly as sin. He has obtained the following defects: lumped forehead incorporating sticky hair whisping, stupid expression.

PAINTER   What do you make of that, then?

CUT TO

BRITISH INFORMATION BOARD — SAFETY IN THE HOME

Titles same as they ever were . . . this week, however, over a picture of a nice semi-detached house, the title reads . . .

Safety in the home

Scene One

We are inside the kitchen of a three-bedroom semi. It is not a fitted, MFI type affair, but rather a kitchen that your ma and pa might've had that revolves around a kitchen table. At this stage we are recommending a green and creamy yellow colour scheme. Bob is sat at the table. Vic is stood by him, hitting him full on in the face with a copper frying-pan. It must be the case that it appears that Bob is being hit very, very hard indeed . . . perhaps the new backward foil might help here . . . If no one knows where to get it, we might be able to help . . . we've got a couple of names.

CRAIG TOWNSEND & LAURA MAYHEW   Anywaysup.

VOICE-OVER   Hey, you.

VIC & BOB   Who . . . us?

VOICE-OVER   Yes, you, are you brutally pounding that man in the face with an iron pan?

VIC   Yes.

VOICE-OVER   Are you aware that such behaviour can lead to permanent damage?

BOB   *(who is hideously disfigured, i.e. one raised and one lowered eyeball, extremely flattened nose and lower lip pulled severely to one side, allowing hideously swollen tongue to pop out. A general redness of the skin is apparent, as is a still-lit cigarette in his mouth and a spider hanging from his fringe)* No!

VOICE OVER   Well, it can . . . just look at the state of that pan. . . it's ruined.

Vic examines the pan. There are traces of eyeball, blood, teeth, cigarettes and spiders on the pan's surface.

VIC   Sorry.

VOICE-OVER   Use the right tool for the job . . . like, er, that German photographer's iron beard.

We see a previously unseen German photographer seated at the table wearing a heavy iron beard. Vic pulls the beard off very easily and matter of factly recommences beating Bob.

VOICE-OVER   That's better.

GERMAN PHOTOGRAPHER (PAUL WHITEHOUSE)   Ein, zwei, drei, fier, funf . . . funf

deutschmark for a penny chew . . . but I am Helmut Newton . . . surely I get a discount?

Scene Two

Jack and Eric have removed the floorboards from one of the rooms in their home and removed some of the joists in order to install a revolving 5 ft Return of the Jedi *badge that Jack lies on and it revolves.*

VOICE-OVER   Hey, you!

J&E   What, us?

VOICE-OVER   Yes, you . . . is that your underfloor rotating *Return of the Jedi* badge?

J&E   Yes!

VOICE-OVER   Don't you know that revolving images from space trilogies can cause sudden outbreak of Puff the Magic Dragon fever in the neighbourhood?

J&E   No!

VOICE-OVER   Well, it can, so turn it off.

Scene Three

Eric has installed himself under a bath so that he can observe the bather through the overflow hole. In the bath is an overweight man who is the mayor of the village. He is smoking a pipe.

VOICE-OVER   Hey, you!

MAYOR   What, me?

VOICE-OVER   No, you!

Eric with a pleading face and waving hand pleads to the voice not to give the game away.

VOICE-OVER   Oh, all right.

CUT TO   Outside bathroom where Jack is in the corridor.

VOICE-OVER   Does your friend realize that

underbath mayor observation booths can lead to an outbreak of Mary, Mungo and Midge fever in the council chamber?

JACK   No.

VOICE-OVER   Well, it can, so tell him to stop it.

Scene Four

Eric and Jack are nicely set in a double bed with their pyjamas on. Eric is just turning to switch off the bedside lamp.

VOICE-OVER   Hey, you!

VIC & BOB   What now?

VOICE-OVER   Are you going to bed?

VIC & BOB   Yes.

The light is turned off (or extinguished).

Pause a while.

VOICE-OVER   Budge up, let me get in.

VIC & BOB   Oooh ah . . . why don't you just leave us alone . . . get off!

We then see in the darkness a red amplifier light go on, followed by the unmistakable hum of a jack lead plugged into an electric guitar with its volume control on too high.

A heavy rock chord rings out.

VIC & BOB   Oh God, not again, that's it.

There then follows in the darkness a series of shootings. Each flash of gunfire picks out the images of the participants in the battle.

1. Jack is crouched on bed with shotgun firing directly at Mr Voice-over (see drawing) who is lying in bed with his head visible above the sheets.

2. Mr Voice-over is pinned against a wall with Eric shooting him in the firing squad stance.

3. Jack is firing in the sniper style from on top of the wardrobe.

4. Eric is firing in the Rambo style indiscriminately around the room.

5. Etc. etc. with various unrealistic shooting stances.

The room goes silent.

VOICE-OVER   Hey, you!

A single shot is heard . . . the rock and roll voice over main is dead . . . long live the deep blue sea and the herrings therein.

**CELEBRITY GUEST:
JUAN NELLIE THE ELEPHANT**

Bob is seated at the celebrity interview area.

BOB   Ladies and gentleman, tonight's final guest is the star of the Cuban soap opera *Bola Bola Bola*. Yes, please welcome . . . Juan Nellie the Elephant.

Enter Juan Nellie the Elephant (Vic). He wears 70s white suit, a brown and cream shirt with large round collar and a large knotted yellow tie. He has tinted Simon Bates style glasses. He has a black side parted afro wig, long thick sideburns and a thick blue moustache.

BOB   Thank you for coming. Now, Juan, has the success of *Bola Bola Bola* in this country surprised you?

JUAN   *(in Cuban accent)* Well, no, not really, you know it has a strong storyline and much of the characters are very strong. *(in George Formby voice and to the audience)* Combined fridge freezer, lovely. *(Back to Cuban accent)* Beautiful setting and, of course, beautiful women.

BOB   Is this your first visit to England?

JUAN (George Formby voice) Yes, ducks. It's my very first time in Europe. The Zanussi, love . . . Yes, it's a nice machine . . . Did you take out the extended warranty? You did. Good, it's a bit more expensive but you're buying peace of mind really. (Cuban accent) I am enjoying my stay in your country and I hope to see Amen Corner, Dave Dee, Dozy, Beaky, Mick and Tich and Marmalade on the same bill.

BOB Have you had a chance to see any of the British soap operas?

JUAN (Cuban accent) No, for I have been so busy trying to get tickets for the Edison Lighthouse, Hollies and Tremeloes . . . Wow, what a bill! (George Formby voice) Braun twin speed hairdrier, love . . . very nice . . . You might find you seldom use the slow speed though. How much did you pay, love . . . really . . . well, I could have done it a couple of quid cheaper . . . Bear me in mind next time. (Cuban accent) Yes, in my country such artists are rarely found on the same bill.

BOB What bands are popular in Cuba at the moment?

JUAN (Cuban accent) Pah, indie rubbish: Happy Mondays, New Fast Automatic Daffodils . . . Or the New Fads . . . Boxer. (George Formby voice) Food processor . . . Mmm, yes, so you're an idle wife . . . personally, I wouldn't bother, love, they're a bugger to clean. (Returns to Cuban accent but, hold on, isn't it slightly impaired by Halifaxonian tones?) Cabaret Voltaire (Oh, oh it's becoming pure Halifaxonian meets Skiptonian!) Max Jaffa, Mantovani . . . Oh, yes, Mantovani . . . I love the sweeping strings, gorgeous. You like him, love . . . But use a nice midi stack system with CD and a loudness button to enhance those sweeping strings . . . I've got one that would do you in the van . . . nice Tandy . . .

BOB (quickly interrupting the sales pitch) Hold on, Vic, hold on.

VIC What is it, ducks? Do you want one? I've got two but one's shopsoiled. Could knock a bit off.

BOB (firmly) Vic, stop it right now. Look, you were meant to be a Cuban actor. You looked good . . . the hair, the blue tash . . . smart. So what's all this electrical goods salesman nonsense?

VIC I'm sorry, Bob. But I told you, I was no good as a Cuban.

BOB But, Vic, we were that far from convincing people that we had a decent guest on for once.

Bob gets up, walks over to Vic and punches him in the face.

VIC Away, Bob, who's the most interesting, a Cuban or a home appliance salesman?

BOB A Cuban.

Gets up walks over to Bob and punches him in the face.

VIC Wrong.

Vic and Bob sit silently glowering at each other and then commence to throw handfuls of party snacks at each other from dishes on the coffee table. As they do so a voice-over (BBC Oxbridge) indicates what variety of fun party snack is being thrown.

VOICE-OVER Salted peanuts, Twiglets, little square Cheesy Bites, Bombay Mix, Iced Gems, Mini Baby Beets.

VIC Come on, we'll solve this by song.

Cue music to:

SONG: 'LET'S HAVE A LOOK AT IT'

I love the smell of Fidel Castro,
Ah yes, but he'd be lost without his Flymo,

But electrical appliances don't promote banana
   growth.
Good point, Bob, let's have a look at them.
Pick a bunch, Vic, let's have a sniff of them.
Smells good, Bob, let's look a little bit more.

CUT TO   A 40-year-old heavily breasted Mrs
Beaton type who alternately lifts each breast in
rhythmn to the tone raising middle eight 'BUM
DIDDY BUM DIDDY BUM DE BUM DE BUM'.
(NB She simply mouths the bum diddys which
have been pre-recorded by a Red Indian male.)

Cuban coffee beans there are none finer,
But those beans are useless without my electric
   coffee bean grinder,
But, Vic, what do you think these Cuban heels are
   for?
Good point, Bob, let's have a cup of it.
Sorry, Vic, I don't have a kettle here.
Never mind, Bob, I've got one under this beard.

On display is a full size Castro head with beard.
Vic pulls out a small electric kettle from under the
beard. The Castro head then mouths the 'bum
diddy' sequence with Red Indian voice.

Bob, you know you're right, I see your vision.
Good, you're ready now to embrace communism.
Yes, I'll open up my own private prison,
Cheap labour equals cheap consumer goods,
We'll smoke cigars in our mansion in the woods.
Come along now, what are we waiting for?

[Have a havana!]

THE BRA MEN: 'AT THE ROADSIDE TEA STALL'

Pat and Dave are seen pulling into a lay-by in
their brown Triumph Dolomite to visit a roadside
tea caravan. They are at the counter which is
being attended by a fat, greasy, sweaty,
miserable, sullen po-faced creep (Charlie Higson).

DAVE   Two teas, please.

CHARLIE   What size cup . . . small or large?

Then either

1. Dave simply gives an embarrassed and coy look
to Pat.

or

2. **DAVE**   (coy, but at the same time thrusting his
breasts upwards towards the attendant) Why,
can you not tell?

SHOW

INTRODUCTION

We were thinking of a very beautiful young woman wearing an extremely tight peach négligé and nothing else but all we got was a 57-year-old moonshine salesman from Louisiana. Yeah, so he was wearing a négligé and, yes, it was peach but hot diggidy dang did he really have to be wearing an 'I Luv Sarsaparilla' eyepatch?

Anyway we had spent a lot of money on this party négligé-gram and as soon as we saw him we knew little diabetic Chris was going to be not only very disappointed but also tremendously annoyed . . . let us explain:

You see, Chris was the type of kid who had always had everything on a plate, he was PAMPERED and SPOILT and he always got his own way, so when the moonshine salesman turned up instead of the lovely young girl he turned to his mom and yelled out for all to hear, 'I HATE YOU, MOM. AND THAT'S WHY I SHOT PA.' The room was stunned into silence as for the first time the people of Brownsville, Durham heard the real story surrounding the untimely death of Mr Richard Carlisle.

It was August 1964 when Mr Carlisle set off to fetch the apple of his eye, little Chris . . . Sorry, that's all there was on the piece of paper we found. The only other record of the events that unfolded that night is the notebook of PC Peeky the Copper That Wears a Bow Tie . . .

OPENING TITLES

The following voice-over will require the word FOG to be gradually emphasized via the gift of echo. It is for insertion at the commencement of Show 6.

Voice-over

Fog . . . man's greatest fear

Fog . . . harbourer of vile and noxious fumes

Fog fog . . . the cloak of death

Fog fog fog . . . friend of the POW escapee

Fog fog fog fog . . . malevolent benefactor of the Raffles type character

Fog fog fog fog . . . the curtain of sin

Fog fog fog fog . . . curse of the milkroundsman

Fog fog fog fog . . . the sailors' nemesis

Fog fog fog fog . . . the patron saint of the luminous clothing industry

That was until the invention in 1961 by Sir John Betjamin of the Foghorn (insert foghorn blast), enemy of fog fog fog. So successful was this invention that in 1967 the supergroup The Who swooped down from the moon and declared, 'I can see for miles and miles.'

Now welcome on fog-free TV . . . ladies and gentlemen, Reeves and Mortimer.

Suggested images to accompany v/o for show 6

1 *Swirling fog.*
2 *May the swirling fog be injected with greenness to suggest noxious fumes.*
3 *May a horned man appear within the fog.*
4 *May a POW camp searchlight beam up the fog, revealing briefly a scurrying figure.*
5 *May we return to a blast of thick swirling fog.*
6 *May a shadowy figure wearing a cape and top hat appear within the fog and doff his top hat.*
7 *May a shrouded lady of the night appear from within the fog and say 'Five bob to you, sir.'*
8 *May the sound of an electric milk float be heard to crash and then may a milkman be heard to say 'bloody fog!'*
9 *May the clanging sound of a ship's bell be*

heard briefly and then the words 'how did that milk float get on the ship?'

10 *May a cyclist with luminous belt and armbands ride through the fog and smile at the camera.*

11 *The fog suddenly clears to reveal a man wearing a great big black overcoat, no trousers, a pair of yellow Turkish curl up at the front to form a loop slippers, a green pixie's hat and table-tennis eyes. He has 15 Bic biros sticking out of his mouth. He is operating a piece of equipment that says foghorn on it. This machine is simply a painted cardboard box with a big funnel stuck in one end and a Morris 1100 hand starter winch crank in the other.*

12 *A still of either The Who or Bill Withers.*

SONG: 'TRAPPED IN MY FLAT'

I haven't left my flat for over three months
and the council erected an iron door
an easy mistake for the council to make
but the grilles on the windows are an eyesore.

I shouted out the window
I shouted out the door
I tried to tunnel out through the kitchen floor
I pushed lighted paper through the letter-box
but nobody saw because of the iron door.

Trapped in my flat
only my memories for company
trapped in my flat
hoping someone will come and rescue me.

I phoned up the council, they'd destroyed my file
clearly the staff there presumed I'd died
it's an easy mistake for the council to make
there was nothing they could do but they
    apologized.

There's nothing I can do and that's a simple fact,
but to sit here until they demolish these flats

so till then I stand in my attic space
trying to attract the attention of passing planes.

Trapped in my flat
only my memories for company
trapped in my flat
hoping someone will come and rescue me.

Repeat first verse – but up one tone and more rousing.

VIC & BOB

Vic and Bob settle down at their desk and commence telling their quickfire funny jokes . . .

VIC Bob, I've just spoken to a lad who's come back from the Gulf.

BOB Was it dangerous?

VIC Much the same as any other garage.

BOB I honestly, truly, find that very amusing indeed.

VIC Thank you, Bob . . . I think I do too.
Oh, Bob, do the clocks go back tonight?

BOB Yes. I told you we should have kept up the payments.

VIC Excellent, very good indeed. I say, Bob, you won't catch me queuing up for the sales.

BOB Why not?

VIC Because, Bob, we don't have a boat.

BOB That's simply a very funny piece of humour. I had to go to Guy's Hospital last night.

VIC Why was that?

BOB Well I'm not going to the girls' hospital, am I?

VIC That's it . . . that's the one . . . la pinnacle. *(Performs the specialist Italian hand movement that an Italian mayor might use after tasting a superb pasta sauce and declaring it the winner in the Mussolini memorial pasta competition.)*

Vic and Bob then both perform this hand movement whilst making the following comments: 'Sarsaparilla'; 'Hercule Poirot's murder casebook closed'; 'A little cheese shop in Cardiff'; 'Delightful donkey jacket, sir'.

NO MORE LONELY NIGHTS

BOB *(looking at Vic's hands)* Haven't you got ladylike hands.

Close-up of a lady's beautiful hands wearing lovely rings and bracelets.

VIC Thank you.

BOB Mm . . . really lovely . . .

VIC Bob, it's the last show and soon you'll be attending interviews for other jobs.

BOB I know, and I'm useless at interviews.

VIC I know, Bob, remember I interviewed you for this job. *(Holding up picture of Bob's face stuck on the body of another or alternatively an actual photo of Bob in quite sad clothing.)* Now, Bob, what sort of work are you looking for?

BOB Well, I've got an interview coming up as foghorn operator for P & O Ferries. I know it doesn't sound much, but you know you're not restricted to just one ferry . . . not, you're more of a roving hornsman.

VIC No, Bob, sounds right up your street . . . Blowing your own horn and creeping about in fog . . . Mind you, Bob, maybe you're aiming too high. Let me ask you a few questions on the work

of the ferry foghornsman . . . One, what do the initials P & O stand for?

BOB Post Office.

VIC Oh no, Bob, it's Port Orthority.

BOB Blast.

VIC That was the answer to me second question – what does a foghorn do – I'll have to ask you another one now. Question two. Now, Bob, the traditional ingredients for a ploughman's lunch are what ?

BOB Erm, bread, cheese, pickle . . . foghorn?

VIC Wrong, wrong, wrong. The traditional ploughman's lunch comprises courgettes, toffees and, er . . . vinegar. Question three – and, Bob, let's be honest, if you don't get this you're clearly applying for the wrong job – now you're on the Dover to Calais ferry for a one-week shift. What are the three most important items on the ship?

BOB Well, the foghorn of course, radar and . . . the anchor.

VIC Oh grow up, will you. The three most essential items for any cross-channel voyage are: limes for scurvy, barrels of rum and, er . . . vinegar.

BOB Oh blow. And are these the sort of questions I'll be asked at an interview?

VIC Yes, of course. Look, Bob, I don't think it's the job for you.

BOB Problem is, Vic, the CV I've written was tailored to that job. *(Produces CV from his pocket. It is in the form of an elaborate scroll with an impressive wax seal and beautiful gold and red ribbon.)*

VIC *(taking CV from Bob)* Ah, yes, previous experience . . . this is the important section. Let's see what you've put . . . *(reading from the scroll)* In 1963 I was presented with the ceremonial foghorn used by Horatio Hornblower at the Battle of the Big Horn. In 1973 I wrote the music for the hit album *Fog on the Tyne* and also ghost-wrote the best selling Stephen King novel *The Fog*. Since then I have written songs for artists such as Goldie Hawn, Bryan Ferry, Paul Anka, Bruce Hornsby . . . and Trevor Horn.

At this point Vic's voice fades to the rear as Bob delivers the following aside to camera:

BOB   Isn't he pathetic. That's not my proper CV. I know he's applied for that foghorn job. He's desperate for it . . . he loves foghorns, he's a foghorn bore. I knew he'd try to put me off the job . . . he's so transparent. Anyway, I'll go along with it just to keep the little weed happy.

Fade back to Vic continuing his reading of the CV.

VIC   The Admiralty regularly dine on my cream horns, yours sincerely . . . Hey, Bob, you haven't even signed it.

BOB   What's the point, I'm not going to get the job, am I?

VIC   No, I don't suppose you will get it. But cheer up, every crowd has a silver lining and what better way to beckon in a long period of unemployment than the Uncle Peter band . . .

CUT TO

UNCLE PETER BAND

The Uncle Peter Band perform a song in their usual habitat and dress.

'Looks Like I'm Going Back Again'
(R. Stewart & R. Wood)

I want to be erotic
I want to be in *Tatler*
I want a cup of tea.

At this point Uncle Peter stops playing his drums and delivers the Charlie Chick story about a man with his eye severely injured who is not bothered whether he has a cup of tea or not. This story will end with the phrase 'I want a cup of tea' at which point Uncle Peter commences drumming again and the song continues . . .

I want a cup of tea
I want to know what tofu is
I want to go on the mad mouse
And I want to do it now.

At this point Peter gets up from his drums, picks up his microphone and becomes a proper light entertainment singer, you know, like Jack Jones or Englurberg Humpromink . . . and with his most sincere light entertainment singing voice to a sentimental tune like 'Honey' by Bobby Goldsboro. He commences singing to the piano accompaniment and walks to a high singing stool centre stage. The song goes as follows:

But most of all what I want
is you back by my side.

When will you be coming home,
and when can I stop crying?

'Cos, Daddy, I miss you
and, Daddy, I care
and I long to be with you
on the arm of your chair . . .

At this point Peter cracks up and begins to weep uncontrollably as he repeatedly says, 'DON'T SEND ME BACK'.

Vic and Bob plus 2 men and 2 women (please see picture enclosed for men and their dress . . . the women should be of similar type) gather round Peter's chair. They are all holding sherry glasses and eating little fairy cakes with cherries on top.

The camera hasn't seen them walk over to Peter but rather pulls back from a close-up of Peter's anguish to reveal them stood there listening to Peter. Vic and Bob tell the pianist to stop and tell the two men and two women to clear off. They then ask Peter what the matter is . . .

PETER Show's finished. I'm going to have to go back. *(Etc., etc. and getting increasingly distraught.)*

BOB As you can see, Vic, the prospect of long-term redundancy can cause great emotional distress.

VIC Yes, and sometimes family break-up, spiralling debt and, of course, occasional, suicide.

BOB Thank God there's sufficient of us who still care *(indicating themselves)*.

VIC And two people, Bob, who've never stopped caring are Otis and Marvin — let's see if they've got any advice for Uncle Peter . . .

CUT TO

OTIS AND MARVIN

They are situated in their usual spot, just watching ships come in and go out again.

OTIS Hello, Vic, Hello, Peter . . . Yes, we're still sat here watching the ships come in *(turns to Marvin for Marvin to finish the line but Marvin is drinking Tennents Super lager and couldn't care less, so simply turns away from Otis)*. Oh, Marvin . . . and watching them go out again. We're looking forward to a consignment of Mazola that's due in today, aren't we, Marvin? Marvin!

MARVIN *(sarcastically)* Oh, I can't wait.

OTIS What is it with you, Marvin? You used to love coming here with me watching the . . .

MARVIN I know, watching ships coming in and

out. We've been here six weeks and only seen one ship. Can't we do something decent for once, like kissing in the back row of the movies with the Drifters and their mates, or just go down the Grapevine and hear a bit of gossip?

OTIS Marvin, you're becoming unconventional in your habits. Now behave and keep a look-out for that Mazola coming in. Now, Vic, how can I help?

VIC It's Uncle Peter, Otis. He's having difficulty coming to terms with his imminent redundancy.

OTIS Well, a temporary solution for Peter might be to enrol for volunteer work here at the docks as good people are always needed to sit here watching the ships coming in . . .

MARVIN *(aggressively interrupting)* Yeah, and going out again, we all know. If he wants to know about depression he should come and spend six weeks sitting with this joker.

OTIS Marvin, really. Your attitudes are becoming increasingly unorthodox and in a lot of ways independent. Sober up, this is a serious problem.

MARVIN I couldn't give a toss. Serious problem! I want to do some serious drinking . . . *(getting up and starting to dance about)* . . . and get myself some sexual healing . . .

Marvin becomes increasingly more badly behaved and irritating as he taunts Otis to give up watching ships and come with him for a kebab. Otis desperately tries to calm him. It's no good, Marvin is now dancing round like a 4-year-old, waving his arms in the air and shouting 'YEAH YEAH YEAH'. In this new independent state, Marvin accidentally knocks Otis into the sea — a splash is heard — Marvin then sees the Mazola ship coming in, and in his enthusiasm to alert Otis falls in himself . . . leaving the dockside once again tranquil and empty.

VIC   Well, Peter, I hope that's been of some assistance. It's certainly given me a few ideas . . . How about you, Bob?

BOB   I don't know, Vic, I was playing pocket billiards . . . How about you, Peter?

PETER   Missed it. I was playing pocket billiards with Bob.

VIC   Me too.

BOB   *(looking confused, abused, misused and slightly soiled)* Vic, I can't get over how ladylike your hands are.

Close-up of lady's hands handling a lovely Fabergé egg in soft focus.

VIC   Thank you, kind sir.

BOB   Oh, it's nothing. They really are lovely.

VIC   Let's see how Slade are getting on . . .

CUT TO

SLADE IN RESIDENCE

Slade are in their flat as per usual. Dave is sat on a kitchen chair with a white towel around his neck. Jim is kneeling in front of Dave holding a 6-inch diameter Fray Bentos steak and kidney pie, in its tin, in front of Dave's face with a one-foot-long pair of coal tongs.

DAVE   You'd better get this right, Noddy Holder, or you spend the rest of the evening in your room with no Cup-A-Soup.

NODDY   Up a bit, Jim, left a bit, that's it. Now hold still, Mr Hill . . . right . . . biro . . .

Jim hands Noddy a biro and Noddy draws round the outline of the tin on to Dave's face. Unfortunately, the line is skew-whiff. The pie tin is then pulled away revealing the line on Dave's forehead. Dave lets the fringe of his hair fall over the line on his forehead . . you see, Dave is having his hair cut by Noddy and the biro line is the line Noddy will be following with his scissors.

Noddy commences cutting the hair. Don enters the room. No one really notices him. In his right hand he has a kebab in paper that has excess tomato ketchup on it. He is pretending that he has injured his hand.

DON   Aaargh aaaaah.

Nobody responds.

DON   Oooohhh aaaaah.

Nobody responds.

DON   Ooh aah *(louder)*, look, you lot, I've cut me hand off . . . Get a doctor someone.

NODDY   No you haven't, Don, it's a kebab. That's the tenth time you've done that this week. Now behave, I'm cutting Dave's hair.

DON   Oh aye, what's the big occasion then?

JIM   Dave's going next door to complain about their cat doing his wee wees on the marigolds.

From next door and muted through the wall we hear the sound of UB40 (i.e. like the band are practising next door), playing the song 'Red, Red Wine'.

DON   While you're there, Dave, tell them to stop practising in their front room.

Don pulls a picture of airborne Spitfire emerging through cloud. You know the picture . . . Christ, you must have seen it a thousand times . . . and puts his eye to a peephole on the wall that goes through to next door.

CUT TO   Next door front room as seen through peephole. We see the seven members of UB40, in the nude, playing 'Red, Red Wine'. Don replaces picture and bangs on the wall saying:

DON   Shut up, you lot!

Unfortunately, he has banged on the wall with the hand holding the kebab and has therefore covered the wall in cheap meat and tomato ketchup.

DAVE   Oh, Don, what have you done to me nice clean wall. It's a good job it's vymura or you'd be joining Noddy Holder in his room with no Cup-A-Soup. Now go and get a J Cloth and clean it up.

DON   Oh, I don't know where you keep them. You know where they are, Jim, go and fetch one.

Jim starts to get up. Dave stops him.

DAVE   You stay right where you are, young man, or you'll be joining Noddy Holder and Don Powell in your room. You'll find that there's a J Cloth hanging on the washing-line.

NODDY   Hold on a minute. You said me and Don would have to go to our room without Cup-A-Soups, so what's so special about Jimmy?

DAVE   Just you shut up and concentrate on what you're doing.

We see close-up of the final cut on the fringe of Dave's hair and hot diggidy dang, it's skew-whiff and there is much hair on Dave's face.

NODDY   Right, there you are, Dave, it's finished.

DAVE   How does it look, Jimmy Lea? Is the bend even?

JIMMY   *(trying to disguise his amusement)* Yeah, it's bostin', Dave.

Noddy is behind Dave doing the Slade finger point at his head and stifling his laughter.

DAVE   What's the big joke, Noddy Holder?

NODDY   *(in high-pitched voice of innocence)* Nothing, Dave, nothing.

DAVE   *(to Jimmy)* Well, what are you laughing at then?

JIM   *(in high-pitched voice of innocence)* Nothing, Dave, nothing.

DAVE   Right, you lot, I'm going next door to see about this messy cat weeing on me marigolds, so let's not have any mischief or you know what will happen.

NODDY   Yeah, no Cup-A-Soup, apart from teacher's pet, Jimmy. *(Slade finger point delivered to Jimmy by Noddy.)*

Dave leaves scene via front door.

JIMMY   You shut your cakehole, muttonchops.

NODDY   You shut it or I'll give you a bit of that *(holding fist towards Jimmy)*.

JIMMY   *(squaring up to Noddy)* Yeah, you and whose army?

NODDY   Hold on, let's see how Dave's getting on next door.

Noddy goes over to Spitfire picture to look through the peephole into next door.

NB *Do you remember a kebab being punched against the very same wall and leaving what appeared to be bloodstains? Well, this 'blood' has now mysteriously formed itself into the words 'HELP', but please, please, please not in too obvious a way. Obviously the house is haunted, probably by Terry the tortoise, the ghost tortoise.*

Camera takes Noddy's perspective as he stares into UB40's front room. They have now been joined by Dave. The shot should reflect the stifled view and the sound should be slightly muffled. We hear the following conversation . . .

DAVE   Right, I want to have a word with you lot about your cat having its wee wees on my marigolds.

Some of the band start to titter.

BAND MEMBER   What are you talking about? We haven't got a cat. It got killed by a rat in the kitchen.

All the band start laughing.

DAVE   Oh, very funny joke, isn't it? My marigolds getting weed on. You wouldn't like it if I came and had a wee in your red, red wine.

BAND MEMBER   No, Mr Hill, it's not that, it's your fringe.

DAVE   What about it?

Dave looks in mantelpiece mirror.

BAND MEMBER   Anyway, Mr Hill, it's your mate Don who's been piddling on the marigolds. We can see him from our bedroom window.

DAVE   Right, that lot are for it now.

We see Noddy and Dave quickly move away from the peephole and adopt 'innocent'-looking stances.

NODDY   Oh God, we're for it. Here quick, he's coming back.

Dave enters angrily through front door.

DAVE   *(to Noddy and Jim)* Right, you two, bed now and no Cup-A-Soup.

NODDY   *(finger-pointing Jim)* Not even for Jimmy?

DAVE   Bed.

Enter Don who is fiddling with his trouser flies, having obviously just had a wee in the garden. Dave clearly realizes this fact.

DAVE   So it was you. Get to bed with your brothers.

DON   What about my Cup-A-Soup?

DAVE   Now!

Dave sits down in easy chair. We can hear the muffled sound of someone laughing. Dave looks up at a picture of Laughing Cavalier, which has an extremely obvious peephole in the cavalier's eye and an equally visible eye looking through it at Dave. Dave points up to the picture.

DAVE   And I don't know what you think you're laughing at, Ozzy Osbourne.

Close-up of Ozzy's peephole closing as the muffled laughter abruptly stops.

POCKET BILLIARDS

CUT TO

Vic and Bob are stood centre stage. They both have their hands in their pockets. They have adopted the manner and stance of two blokes on their dinner break with nothing at all to do. We can hear the sound of snooker balls clacking against each other and being pocketed. Suddenly we hear the applause from a crowd that signifies the end of a frame. Bob raises his arm in triumph and shakes hands with Vic in the way that defeated player and victor shake hands when victory is being conceded. FOR THEY HAVE JUST COMPLETED A GAME OF POCKET BILLIARDS.

After shaking hands Vic and Bob return to the subject of the vacancy with P & O Ferries for a foghorn operator . . .

VIC   I'm pleased you won that game, Bob, 'cos you must be really down in the dumps . . . you know, after finding out that you're underqualified . . . you know, not quite bright enough . . . for the foghorn operator's job.

BOB   Thanks, yes, it's helped a bit. I'm sure it will go to the right person in the end.

VIC   *(smugly)* Yes, I think it probably will . . . Hey

Bob, anyway, I saw a job on the cork noticeboard out the back that would be right up your street.

BOB What is it?

VIC Come along . . . I'll show you . . . (Vic begins to lead Bob off stage then turns to declare) In the mean time, here's Adrian Marsh.

THE DISTANCE GAME
HOSTED BY ADRIAN MARSH

Opening shot is of Lord Simon Crow. He is stood to the side of the distance game arena. He is dressed in a second-hand brown suit that is slightly too small, white socks and Jesus sandals.

He is aged between fifty and sixty years. He is a tall man, ideally 6' 4". He has prominent, protruding teeth. His hair, whatever the style, is greasy and unkempt. He has a little pencil moustache and wide crazy eyes. There is a suspicion that he has, in the recent past, been vaguely involved in the disappearance of livestock and an unlicensed pond burial. This suspicion is backed up by the presence of various stains on his suit, including one particularly fresh-looking one consisting of a 4" dribble of Silvikrin creamy hair conditioner on his lapel. He is also wearing a number of rings.

Lord Simon Crow stares almost menacingly at the audience and then proceeds to outline an expanding air circle with his pointing finger (with one long, dirty fingernail). When the circle reaches its perable, he makes a sad and vague ZZ Top style pointing motion to the centre of the stage.

Enter Adrian Marsh (Vic) over short musical intro. Adrian is aged thirty-five. He has been a working-class hippy for too long. His mind, speech, demeanour, conduct and morals have become blurred and stretched by indulgence in anti-depressants, beefburgers and Pernod. In a vague way he speaks in the way that a drunken Mick Jagger might do.

He is dressed in a khaki safari suit with nothing underneath. He has a small lady's black 1950s short high-cropped wig, the kind you might find in a thrift or dime store . . . hey, hey, hey. His suit is besmirched with the memories of many fats. He is smoking a fag. He wears cheap towelling sports socks and Jesus sandals. He is wearing a pair of horn-rimmed glasses.

Over the short musical intro, Adrian attempts to sing in a unique style.

ADRIAN It's the distance in me
I hear you say
Don't let anyone tell you anything different
Babs
Until you've played the distance game.

My name's Adrian Marsh and this is the distance game. Right, now this is what's going to happen, right. Now listen, these guys are coming on. Like one after the other . . . and they're going to try different new ways of like moving themselves over distances.

Now to assist me there's a panel, right, who will judge like decide, right, who has gone the best distance with everything taken into account, you know, everything, you know.

Let me introduce the guys on the panel.

The panel are behind a table. They are each covered with a dustsheet. Adrian removes the dustsheets as he introduces each individual member of the panel.

Panellist one is seated. He is of normal appearance except that he holds out before him, in the manner of an arm wrestler, a beautiful, but obviously oversized, walnut.

ADRIAN This guy, right, like his hand's not normal like . . . it's like, I dunno, a walnut or something . . . listen, man, don't let anyone tell you it's not a walnut, man . . .

Panellist two is seated. he is a partially scaffolded lady's man. His cheeks are one foot wide on either side and each cheek has a little bell on its tip.

ADRIAN This man, right, he's partially scaffolded right, and I've heard, right, that you're a bit of a lady's man, right.

In response to this, the partially scaffolded man rings his two little cheek bells in agreement.

Panellist three is a small man dressed as a guardsman and wearing a busby. Behind him and a good way behind him, mind, is Susan Nelson. She is a dark-haired, 30-year-old woman who has brought up a family of three boys, and the strain is beginning to show. One interesting manifestation of this is a 7 ft light and flimsy breast. This elongated breast is hanging over Albert the Guardsman's busby with the nipple resting on his nose, causing Albert the guardsman a degree of irriation. Albert finds temporary relief from this by blowing the breast away from his face using the protruding jaw upward fringe waft technique.

ADRIAN This guy, right . . . this is one of those guys, right, who guards the like palace . . . and he can't move or nothing . . . hey, look at this, man, a boob . . . and a beautiful boob . . . don't let anyone tell you that you're not a beautiful lady, 'cos you are . . . right?

So that's the like panellists, right, and like let's have the first guy going to play the distance game . . . look, there he is.

CUT TO

The competition area. Not much really. A large suspended ruler graded in feet up to 20 feet and a starting-line represented by a drawing of a cross section of a large dog eating cakes.

Reading and waiting at the starting-line is contestant number one. He is sat in a galvanized dustbin with his head sticking out. He has a beard made entirely out of pork. He has a smaller rubber model red sink plunger sprouting from his brain and protruding through his forehead. He wears a light brown woman's push-back wig. His name is Amanda Withington. On the side of the bin in white paint are the words 'No 75. A Withington'.

ADRIAN Hi, guys.

AMANDA WITHINGTON Hi, Adrian, man.

ADRIAN Wow, that's some bucket, guys.

AMANDA WITHINGTON It's a dustbin, man.

ADRIAN No . . . strange, man. Right, what strange object have you brought me, guys?

Amanda Withington hands Adrian a very ordinary white tea cup.

ADRIAN Wow, higho impacto . . . strange brew, guys . . . right, guys, let's see how far you can go.

Cue drum roll from the tall, greasy man at side of stage we mentioned earlier who now has a drum round his neck.

Amanda begins to suck in air and unleashes a powerful manly sneeze, the after-effects of which vibrate his lips before sending him gently backwards 14 ft.

Adrian follows the bin in the manner that a curling referee might do so. He marks the distance with some toilet paper pulled out of his pocket. Adrian returns to starting-line where second contestant is ready and waiting to play the distance game.

This contestant is a nice realistic dummy. You know, not a shop mannequin, but a padded and clothed one of the type that Benny Hill might have used to drag behind a speeding horse. The dummy is casually laid on the floor with its head on the starting-line. It is dressed in a white suit with black shirt and white tie. He is wearing a very obvious black, side-parted wig. His head is a male mannequin's head that has been made up to look like a cockney hard man. The mouth and jaw have been adapted so that it can speak in the manner that a ventriloquist's dummy does. A fishing-line is attached to his wig to enable him to be pulled and one to its arm to enable the arm to be raised.

ADRIAN Wow, so, panel. What do you think and that?

The panel respond as follows:

- *Walnut man waves his walnut*
- *Scaffold man twiddles his bells*
- *Albert the guardsman blows an upward draft to the breast.*

ADRIAN Great stuff. *(spots dummy on floor)* Wow, man, you are so low . . . maximus lowus. *(gets down to speak to him. For some reason Adrian speaks to him as if he was partially deaf)* Why so low, guys . . . can you hear me? Announcethyourself . . . o low one.

CARL Carl Peters, my son.

ADRIAN Right, Carl. What strange thing have you brought for me, guys?

CARL What do you make of this boy? *(handing Adrian a very ordinary spoon)*

ADRIAN Wow, what a mad spoon . . . maximus strangus spoonus. Right, guys, how are you going to make your name in the distance game.

CARL It's like this, see. Me and my family love chilli con carne. I tell you, we love it, the family and me. We love it . . . can't get enough of the stuff. Me and my family that is. We love it . . . the

wife, the kids . . . all the bloody family, we love it, etc, etc.

ADRIAN Slowus downus. Explainy wainy, guys.

CARL Sorry, guv . . . right, it's like this, see . . . I don't know if you can tell like, but I'm wearing a syrup.

ADRIAN *(Touching wig)* Wow realisticus wiggus.

CARL Thanks. Well, my wig here loves chilli con carne. Now I've put a nice dollop of con carne under that silver salver there, and when you expose it, you just watch my Irish go for it . . . do it, son.

Adrian removes a dustbin lid from on top of a pile of con carne (about one stones' worth). This is situated 16 ft down the distance lane. As soon as it is exposed, the dummy moves towards it by use of the nylon wire attached to head. The dummy only achieves a distance of 12 ft, thus failing by 2 ft to take first position.

ADRIAN Good griefus. Let's see what the panel think.

Pan to Panel who are all doing their various specialized movements.

We return to Adrian back at the starting-line. In the background the dummy, who has now been replaced by a real Cockney wearing identical garments, gets up, grabs a handful of con carne, pats it on to his wig saying 'There you go, my son' and exits in the manner that an ancient bison might do on hearing a rumour that a new type of horn is to be used by the adjoining herd.

Here Adrian gets excited and thrilled by the con carne and announces

ADRIAN That has put me in the mood for a beefburger (or hamburger).

Lord Simon Crow brings it and watches Adrian eat it in a realtively slow and quiet manner. RIP.

Competitor three is already available at the starting-line. This is a husband and wife team. They are man and woman. The man is 68 years. The woman with the man is 64 years young.

The woman is laid in a transparent tube prostrate at the starting-line, i.e. lying on the floor in the tube. The man is stood beside her. He is suffering from irreparable skin disorder such that the skin is literally falling off his face as he speaks.

ADRIAN   Right. What strange thing have you guys brought me?

WOMAN   *(pressing tomato against observation window)* Mmnnggjtysed.

ADRIAN   *(opening hatch)* I couldn't hear you, guyus . . . whatus sayus?

WOMAN   *(now free to speak clearly)* Mmnnggtysed.

ADRIAN   Strange red fruit . . . this fruit must hold the strangest memories for you, sir . . . Are you married to this low lady?

MAN   Yes, for thirty-six years.

ADRIAN   . . . ing hell . . . so make your name on the distance game, brother strange.

MAN   *(in Teeside Pakistani voice)* I put lager in the pipe. It mixes with the Epsom Salts. Pressure builds up behind me wife and she flies out of the end of the tube.

ADRIAN   Wow, play the game, man.

Man pours tin of lager into lager box. We see via the observation window that the tube is filling with Andrews Liver Salts bubbles. A sound is heard representing a terrible build-up of pressure. Finally a large whoosh sound is heard as the foaming liquid bursts out of the end of the tube.

Now depending upon the quality of the bursting water, which presumably is delivered via a huge pressure hose of some sort, Adrian will open the observation window and reveal either a) that the woman has gone or b) that the woman is still there, holding on to her tomato.

ADRIAN   Oh, unlucky lady. So that means the winner is contestant number one with his amazing dustbin.

(Applause.)

ADRIAN   So that's all for this week. But remember, keep sending me strange objects. And don't let anyone tell you you're not beautiful.

DESK SNACKPOT

Vic and Bob are at their desk.

Insert desk Snackpot . . . we hope you understand that we would prefer not to tie our hands at this stage . . . if it is felt that we are being lazy then let's say Bob will hold up a huge length of copper wire and Vic will perform a hilarious caricature of Eddie Cochran beneath it in a vain attempt to lure a Lulu lookalike into his little model chapel made from sweet william pears, and smelling of a thousand saffron rhondells.

Vic and Bob re-enter stage discussing the job on the cork noticeboard . . .

VIC   I'm sorry, Bob. I thought that job was ideal for you.

BOB   Vic, when you said a job on the cork noticeboard I thought you meant there was a job advertised on it . . . I didn't think you meant there was a job going looking after the cork noticeboard and keeping it tidy.

VIC Bob, a thousand apologies but, if you don't mind me saying, what other type of work are you going to get with your lack of skills?

(NB *As an alternative to the above, Bob could have thought he was going to get a job on the SS Noticeboard which sails out of Cork thrice fortnightly . . .)*

And what do you know up pops Ginge off the front of *The Beezer*! No he doesn't. Don't be daft, that was just a joke! Actually it's . . .

LORD CONSOMMÉ AND HIS ASSISTANT LORD CREAM OF TOMATO SOUP

These two are soft-spoken Geordies who have a length of copper piping that proves its own facts. They explain that this length of copper wire is capable of the following:

1. It can teach a stroppy newsagent a lesson when he has pretended not to hear your request for a packet of Polos.
2. Supervise your workforce whilst you remain at home drinking gin . . . Simply place it on a desk at work and just watch sales figures rocket.
3. Put it adjacent to your *A to Z* to determine which roads on your route are one way.
4. Befriend birds in your garden by holding it out in front of you and mimicking birdsong with your whistle.
5. Throw the pipe into your dirtiest room and overnight it will be cleaned and tidied . . . want proof? . . . it's not needed . . . the copper tub proves its own facts.

(NB *These two characters are Vic and Bob at their desk. The only concession made to characterization is . . . MOUSTACHES AND SPECS.)*

Next . . .

Well, that was interesting and we hope you'll find Barry White's new video equally intriguing.

BARRY WHITE'S LATEST HIT VIDEO

This is a pre-recorded video using exactly the same set as the previous Barry White video, featured in Show 3. *The only differences are the following:*

1 *The words of the song (see below)*
2 *A slightly different love fusion groove*
3 *Instead of a person being on the seat opposite Barry there is the copper pipe, feature above, sat opposite him*
4 *On the fire is a big dirty old saucepan of chop suey and in the hearth is a big catering size yellow tin bearing the legend 'CHOP SUEY'*

Everything else, e.g. the meat thrown on the fire, the throbbing chest, the glass of brandy, etc., ARE IDENTICAL.

Are You on Heat, Luv?

I'm looking forward to this evening, love
I've got some chop suey boiling up,
The temperature's rising, oh yes.

Right oh . . . show us your knockers.
That one *(pointing)* and . . . that one.
Oh that's great, man . . .

(to camera)
They call me Mr Huff and Puff
I'm not in a huff
and I'm not a puff.

I just want to make love
to her.

Now where was I, love?
Oh yeah . . . put down that keebab
and put your arms in the air.

Oh that's great, man,
lovely sweaty armpits.

Now, put your hand in that oven glove,
that's right, ease it in real gentle, girl,
now just turn that pan a bit so the chop suey
    heats up
real even.

Oh that's great, man.

(to camera)
I'm just an old owl in love
with this sexy in an oven glove.
The heat from the fire
has made her legs go red.
I'm going to have to run Savlon on them
before we go to bed.
But love all I really want now is tops . . .

*Commences a lunging grab at the lady as
effectively as he can, given the constraints of the
costume and while doing so continues to mutter
words such as 'Come on love . . . Steady
yourself . . . Show us your backside, etc, etc.'*

*Camera pulls back to reveal, firstly, that Barry is
singing to the copper pipe and, secondly, that
Bob has been standing off the set dressed only in
his underpants watching the video being filmed
whilst smoking a fag.*

BOB *(in full Teesside accent)* Now, Barry, man,
behave yourself. You're trying to cop off with a
length of copper pipe, you daft get.

BARRY Don't you insult this lovely sophisticated
lady. Now get out of here before I pop you one.

BOB Suit yourself, Barry, *(looking closely at the
copper pipe)* but that's a copper pipe, son. *(Bob
leaves shaking head and smoking fag.)*

BARRY *(fading)* Sorry about that, love, now
pass us that kitchen roll . . .

CUT TO

GREG MITCHELL'S WIFE, SUSAN

NB *The previous Greg Mitchell may need to be
altered as our intention is to give his appearances
a continuing storyline. This story basically
involves Greg getting set up by Corky who
subsequently is revealed to have been Greg's
wife's lover for the past 15 years. Corky and Mrs
Mitchell run away and Greg is sent to prison for
14 years . . . thus explained we hope the
following Greg Mitchell sketch will make some
sense . . .*

SUSAN *(Greg puppet with brassy blonde tarty
wig, blue eyeliner, lipstick, earrings and a little
brass handbag.)* Hello, Susan Mitchell here . . .
you know, Greg's wife. Well as you probably
know Greg's serving a 14 year stretch for armed
robbery, so I thought I'd take this opportunity in
his absence to announce my engagement to my
longstanding lover, Corky Simpson.

Up pops Corky.

CORKY All right, sweetheart . . . At last we're
together. That nonce Mitchell can rot in hell, ha
ha ha ha.

SUSAN Ha ha ha ha. Yes, we stitched him right
up with that false confession, and the loot's
safely stashed away at 92 The Cedars, Romford,
TS5 7RA . . .

CORKY *(quickly interrupting)* Shut it, you stupid
cow . . . That's my address . . . I don't understand
you women . . . We had it all tied up tight as a
prossy's corset *(insert short, sharp burst of
canned laughter)* Thank you . . . thank you.

SUSAN *(interrupting)* Corky, prossy's corsets
aren't tight.

CORKY Oh, you'd know, wouldn't you . . . get
here. *(They begin to drop below desk with Corky
mumbling his usual inane, vulgar, foul, insipid,
graceless, glittery, creamy, polished but
ultimately obscene expletives.)*

VIC & BOB

Vic and Bob are seated back at the desk. The phone on the desk rings. Vic answers it . . .

VIC Hello . . . ah yes . . . no . . . of course I'll come now . . . Yes *(secretly behind hand)* ask for Mr Hinton, interview room six. Goodbye.

Bob, something's cropped up. That was Mel Gibson on the phone . . . he's in the park on . . . the swings. And he can't get any height so he wants me to go down and give him a couple of shoves. I won't be a minute. Hold the fort while I'm away. *(Hands Bob a small child's toy fort. Vic flees the stage like a frightened man running from a pack of wire wool, or it could be wild wolves? . . . who knows . . . anyway, he's off and he runs in a strange fashion accompanied by the annoyingly loud sound of footsteps.)*

Bob gives camera a look like Richie McCrachan the bass-player out of Taste would give Rory Gallagher when he hits his seventh bum note on the trot during the guitar solo in 'Bullfrog Blues'.

On route Vic runs past four cardboard cartoon characters:

a Mr Napkin Holder
b Miss Bridge of Hair
c Casper the Winepot
d Crackerbarrell the Sheepish Négligé

As he does so they all wave and say, 'Good luck with your interview, Mr Reeves.'

The Interview

Vic then enters through a door marked Interview Room Six. He sits down. The interviewer opposite him on the table is a man in a suit whose head is a giant realistic-looking peach. (NB The peach must have a delved seam to give the impression it could be easily opened and must have a mouth that is capable of mouthing words . . . nowt else, though . . . just the mouth.

PEACH Hello, Mr Reeves. I'm Derek Dougan the ex Wolverhampton Wanderers centre forward, and by strange quirk I now bear the head of a peach . . . but, and it's a big but, when you open the peach there's an underwater worm inside where my brain should be. *(As he says this he pulls open the peach to reveal a small glass tank with a red worm in it on a shelf where his brain should be. Also when he says 'big but' a subliminal one-second picture of a clown with a big 'but' flashes up.)*

Vic stares at the peach and begins to rub his eyes, the way people do when they cannot believe they are seeing a man with a peach's head.

VOICE-OVER *(from the man who will actually be interviewing Vic, see below)* Are you all right, Mr Reeves?

The man who is interviewing Vic is alternative comedian Bob Mortimer, wearing a wig, a liquorice moustache and a pair of glasses. He whistles at the end of every sentence. Vic snaps out of his eye-rubbing activities and now sees before him on the opposite side of the tabel the Interview, Mr Hinton.

VIC Sorry, I thought you were a fruit.

HINTON I beg your pardon?

VIC No, you've got me wrong. I meant a peach . . . er, a seamed peach that, er, *(squirming)* you've got no brain . . . er, you're just a worm . . . Oh, I'm not explaining this very well. *(changing tack and offering handshake)* Anyway, I'm Mr Reeves. I'm here for the foghorn operator's job.

HINTON *(after short pause)* I've got your CV here, Mr Reeves, *(holding up the CV stolen from Bob)* and very impressive it is too. *(Looking at CV and trying hard not to laugh at it.)*

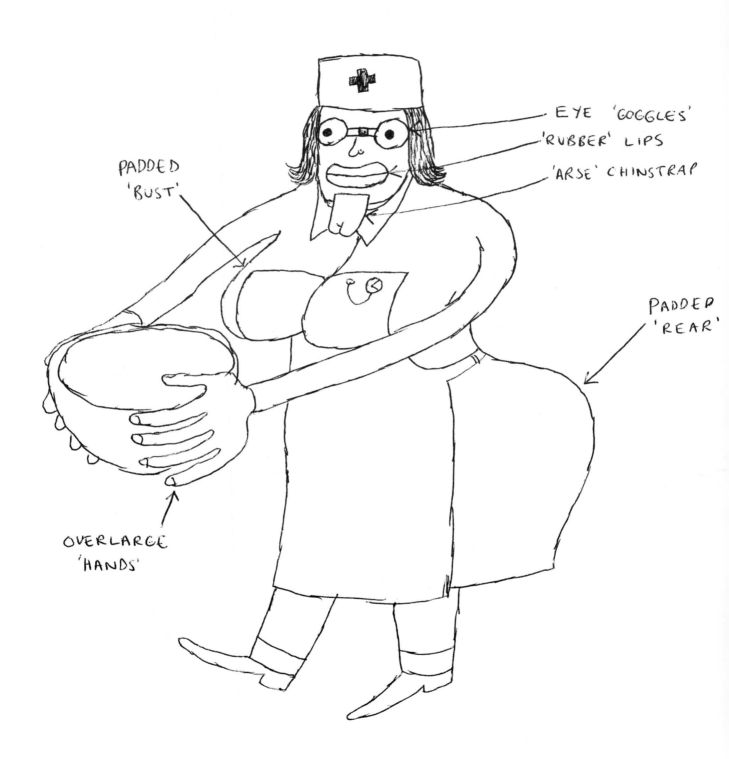

EYE 'GOGGLES'
'RUBBER' LIPS
'ARSE' CHINSTRAP

PADDED 'BUST'

PADDED 'REAR'

OVERLARGE 'HANDS'

VIC *(poncily)* Oh thank you, sir.

HINTON First of all a few questions we're asking all candidates for the job. Firstly, what do the initials P & O actually stand for?

VIC Easy . . . Post Office.

HINTON No, Port Orthority.

VIC I said that.

HINTON No you didn't.

VIC No you're right, that was Bob *(gagging himself as he realizes the error he has made).*

HINTON Secondly, if you were having a moussaka what would you put in it?

VIC I'm sorry, Mr Hinton, but what has that got to do with foghorn operators?

HINTON So you don't know, is that it?

VIC No . . . it's coming . . . er . . . got it . . . Yes . . . pease pudding . . . wool . . . er, Tootie Fruities *(short period of Hinton and Vic looking at each other in a way that suggests Hinton is waiting for one final ingredient)* . . . VINEGAR.

HINTON *(in voice of a teacher patronizing small boy who has completed very simple jigsaw of a clown riding a cockhorse on the wing of Concorde mid Atlantic)* Ooooooooh gooooooodd. *(immediately picks up telephone on desk)* Nurse, Mr Reeves will have a bowl of pease pudding, wool, Tootie Fruities and . . . VINEGAR. *(Puts phone down. Vic looks fearful. Hinton looks smug and self-satisfied. A nurse enters immediately bearing a glass bowl with the aforementioned and somewhat alarming ingredients in it and places it on the table in front of Vic. The nurse (see drawing) is a funny-looking thing.)*

HINTON Thank you, Nurse . . . *(handing her a 3 ft x 1 ft 6" wooden five-pound note painted in a naïve manner)* Here take this wooden five-pound note.

NURSE *(in west country accent)* Oh sir, you're a caution, ain't no denying it.

HINTON *(in west country accent and to camera)* I don't mind telling you, I love that woman like I love my little pink lacy bra. *(As Hinton turns round to face Vic again he catches him with the bowl of food positioned in the pouch of a catapult elastic that has one end attached to a filing cabinet and one end to a sunflower. The bowl flies away accompanied by an elastic twang or boing sound.)* Did you enjoy that?

VIC Yes, thanks.

HINTON Now, reading your CV I see you're presently working on a TV series with that amusing comic Bob Mortimer, and I should inform you in fairness that he has also applied for this job.

VIC He's done what? He told me he wasn't. Look, Mr Hinton, you don't want him for the job . . .

Vic then frantically and arselickingly points out the following appalling characteristics of his rival alternative comedian, Bob Mortimer:

1 He's a bad timekeeper.
2 He always bring his Lego to work ('Hey, Bob, can you fetch me that spanner? No, Vic, I'm too busy with my Lego').
3 He's blind ('Oh where am I? What country is this?'). He wouldn't know . . . that's no good to you, Mr Hinton, is it?
4 He can't tell the difference between stalk and butter. (He doesn't eat butter anyway, just fat pulled straight off animals in his backyard . . . that . . . always makes him sleepy . . . yawn, yawn . . . yeah, yawn.) Mr Hinton, that's no good to you . . . snore, snore, Mr Hinton, that's not the sort of bloke you want.
5 And he's a terrible adulterer . . . yes . . . oh especially with nurses . . . he'd fancy your nurse, Mr Hinton.

6 *Anyway, you wouldn't need a foghorn, Mr Hinton, not with him on board, they would smell him coming a mile off . . . pooo-eee, Mr Hinton . . . pooo-eee, what's that stink, Mr Hinton? That's no good to you, is it?*

Bob takes off his wig, specs and tash thus stopping Vic mid flow . . .

VIC Is it, Mr Hint . . . imer. *(Yes, Vic has clocked that it is Bob who is interviewing him . . . HE HAS BEEN SET UP!)*

VIC Oh it's you. I might have guessed . . . What's going on? . . . Oh I get it . . . I bet there isn't even a job going, is there? *(Uncle Peter walks in slowly.)* Oh very amusing. Oh, Peter, you're his little dogsbody, are you? *(Nurse begins to walk in slowly.)* Oh very funny . . . it's the last show so let's all gang up on Vic and make him look stupid.

More characters from series, e.g. Corky and Susan, a couple of members of Slade gather around Bob as if clearly taking his side in the matter . . . Bob and his cohorts are slightly underlit to suggest a slightly sinister atmosphere: . . . Bob in particular is looking odious and well er . . . you know . . . continental . . . like a foreign chap.

VIC But there's one thing I want to say to you lot . . . *(Vic still seated begins to sing the opening words of the finale. He then gets up and pushes aside the conspirators. When he is past them it is as if he has used them as a gateway to the set for the song.)*

NB *The finale song is staged on the usual set. Various characters contained within the words of the song gradually enter the stage to join Vic. It also is intercut with pre-recorded lines sung by some of the characters Vic and Bob have played in the series in their normal habitat, e.g. Slade in their home, Otis and Marvin on their wall, etc.*

The idea is to film it as a sort of swirling, Quality Street type affair with the camera shifting to pick up the participants' lines as they move hither and thither.

The basic premiss of the song is that the whole series has been a dream and various bizarre aspects of that dream are revealed. The final sad fact revealed is that it is a dream of Vic's and he is having it whilst in a deep and life-threatening coma.

VIC RECOVERS AND SINGS 'DEAR TO ME'

Can you see me sitting near you?
No, I can't, but I can hear you
The joy you bring
In the words you sing
Is dear to me.

Do you remember that little laddie
Abandoned by his daddie
An orphan boy
With just one toy
A teddy bear?

His mother had died in childbirth
This is often the case with smokers
A bulbous head
And on his leg
Cankers.

He lay dying in a hovel
That doubled as a brothel
And in his hand a telegram
From Jesus.

VIC *(Spoken)* And the telegram said

With new joyous big band melody

Get up, get up
Get out of bed
Don't worry about your bulbous head.

So he jumped right up
And put on his jeans
'Cos that little boy

156

BOB *(Spoken)* Was me.

Reprise of big band chorus

Get up, get up
Get out of bed
Clean the teeth in your bulbous head
Clean your specs
Polish your shoes
Comb your hair
Tuck in your shirt
Put on your gloves
And straighten your tie
For tomorrow . . . morrow . . . morrow . . .
You die.

At the end of the song we shift to a hospital bed where a heart machine is beeping away and a life support system is hard at work. The closing titles are run over this image.

CUT TO

Greg Mitchell alone in drip-filled Turkish prison cell. He looks up to a camera and declares:

GREG Hello, Greg Mitchell here. I've just heard the news. The series was just a dream. If that's the case *(changing to deep voice)* then why am I still in here? Oh well, as soon as Mr Reeves hears about this he'll get me out.

We hear the life support system and heart beep go to a constant tone.

Greg is doomed. Vic is dead . . . long live Roxy Music and all their spin-off bands.

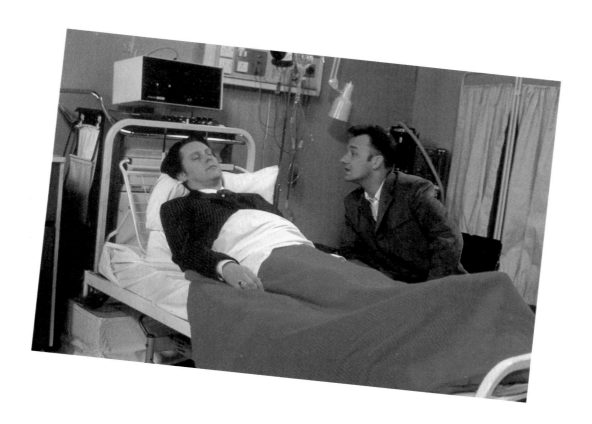

THE END